WORK
LESS
——›«(()»‹——
LIVE
MORE

Paula Brook

Doubleday Canada Limited

Canadian Cataloguing in Publication Data

Brook, Paula, 1952–
    Work less, live more

ISBN 0-385-25654-X

1. Work - Psychological aspects. I. Title.

BF481.B76 1997   158.7   C97–930701–5

Cover design by Bradbury Design
Text design by Heidy Lawrance Associates
Printed and bound in the USA

Published in Canada by
Doubleday Canada Limited
105 Bond Street
Toronto, Ontario
M5B 1Y3

Contents

To my mother, Miriam White

Acknowledgements

I owe thanks to many people, but most of all to the women who welcomed me into their homes and their confidences during research for this book. They were unfailingly generous, patient, and honest. I hope this book serves them well.

In journalistic fashion I credit my sources as I go, saving readers the chore of looking for notes. While this promotes narrative flow, it sometimes short-changes the sources. I'm thinking particularly of Statistics Canada whose social, family, and labour surveys proved an invaluable source of trend analysis. I credit them at least a dozen times in the pages ahead, but probably could have done so a hundred times. Several other support and research organizations provided background materials, including the Vanier Institute of the Family, the Conference Board of Canada's Work and Family Council, and two New York-based organizations: the Family and Work Institute, and Catalyst, a non-profit group advocating workplace change for women.

Doubleday Canada publisher Don Sedgwick first saw the germ of a book in my bag full of wild ideas. Editor Maya Mavjee brought clarity and elegance to the manuscript, Laurie Coulter polished it, and production manager Janine Laporte created a package that combined book format and magazine tone — exactly what I'd been hoping for. My agent, Carolyn Swayze, has been my work/soulmate from the start, seeing the project, and her client, through a dizzying series of starts and near stops.

I have relied greatly on the advice of friends: Cathy Moss, Jennifer Hunter, and Robin Pascoe, Beverly Kort; and the incomparable Girls' Night Out gang, Susan Mendelson, Karen Gelmon, and Miriam Gropper.

And to my family: I'm sorry if I've tested your patience, and made your lives more public than you might have wanted. I promise to keep quiet now, for awhile.

Preface

In the spring of 1996, a year after I left my job as editor-in-chief of a lifestyle magazine, I wrote an article about my decision to quit. It was called "Superwoman Goes Home," and it appeared as the June cover story of *Saturday Night* — a national magazine that is read by a million-odd Canadians, coast to coast. I lost a lot of sleep in the weeks before publication, and not only because the Superwoman title embarrassed me. I tossed and turned over my decision to tell a very personal and not always pleasant story to a wide audience of strangers, many of whom I feared would hate me for it. "Stop the press," I moaned in my dreams. Why was I doing this to myself, I wondered. No one likes a superwoman, least of all a self-professed one. And what makes me so special, just because I quit?

Well, the article came out and my nightmare came true: A lot of people assumed I was advocating quitting — that I was writing not just about my life, but about theirs too. Fortunately, many of them appeared to have no problem with this, and indeed seemed to want to hear more, which surprised me. I was also surprised by the intensity of the reactions to the article, from women *and* men. Several told me the piece was hilarious — the funniest thing they'd read in years. Others said they wept. A male lawyer I know, a senior partner in one of this city's top firms, said he'd photocopied the piece and distributed it to all his colleagues. A female lawyer whom I've never met wrote me a note:

> In your article you managed to touch on every emotion and aspect of the difficult decision a woman faces in leaving a career and the difficulty of balancing the many aspects of a working woman's life. Perhaps it is because misery loves company, but your article created much discussion around the downtown professional community, with copies of it being faxed from one office to the next with comments attached such as "She's saying everything I have been thinking. Wouldn't you like to join her?' ... I keep a copy of the article in my desk drawer at my office and reread it occasionally for inspiration.

I was stunned to see my own little catharsis set off such a storm of public emotion. And I was stunned, again, when invitations started arriving from women who wanted me to "share my message" at conferences and discussion groups, on media panels and talk shows — not just to tell "my story" but to "tell it like it is." It seemed that overnight I'd become Queen of the Quitters: a trailblazer for working women with escape fantasies, a salve for those with stress-fractured egos from too many collisions with glass ceilings, a wake-up call for their employers, plus some kind of unwitting role model for stay-at-home moms who longed to believe they had made the right choice in staying there.

My curiosity was aroused. I had hit a large and sensitive nerve with the Superwoman story, and now I found myself obsessed with dissecting that nerve. So I spent the next several months talking to women — accepting those invitations to speak at seminars and discussion groups, on panels and talk shows. I conducted hundreds of interviews, formal and informal, live and long-distance. I also became a full-fledged mouse potato, electronically chatting with other wired women via e-mail and Internet chatlines, hunting for some way to explain all the frustration, sadness, and pent-up anger I'd encountered since "coming out" as a quitter.

What I found was enough to fill a book, a book of solutions for working women overwhelmed with this business of *balancing* — this challenge of bringing our work lives and home lives back into some kind of healthy, sustainable equilibrium. While my own answer was to quit a job that, as I now see it, was the right job at the wrong time in my life, this would obviously not be every woman's answer. But what I did find in my research were some strong common threads among the questions of working women, which suggested the possibility of common answers. This in itself surprised and pleased me: considering the diverse upbringings, educations, and expectations women bring to their workplaces, not to mention the great variety of work that we do there, it is remarkable how very similar our predicaments actually are, and how equally urgent our desires to solve them.

And this is what has made my research so deeply satisfying. By learning from women who are facing all kinds of work and family issues, I've been able to turn a personal story into a much richer collective journey. The many women you'll meet in the pages ahead have been generous and brave to bare their souls — weeping and laughing out loud while sharing the most personal details of their lives. A few of these women are highlighted in the "Ex-Files" throughout the book (these are first-person accounts of women who have gone through major career transitions). One of them is ex-prosecutor Linda Wrigley, who had the perfect job, a corner office, and flexible hours. But she felt she had to move on when she was finished — when all the passion for putting criminals in prison was spent, and she realized there was a passion deficit at home. In another Ex-File, Anne Mauch tells of life in the crash lane from the perspective of a single, childless woman who hit the wall just as she was hitting her stride, on the eve of her fortieth birthday. What led Mauch, a senior federal bureaucrat, to quit her $75,000-a-year job? Not a cranky husband or out-of-control kids, but the desire to do more with her life by doing less at her job. As former US Labor Secretary Lynn Martin put it, "Women are more aware of what's on the gravestone, which is not 'I worked for IBM.'"

"Mid-life crisis" is a term you won't find in this book. I much prefer the notion of mid-course correction, which is something healthy people do several times in their adult lives. Labelling the sudden and often refreshing immersion in chaos a "crisis" implies that this is a stage in life to be avoided at all costs. (Hang on to that dead-end job! Keep your head down and the blinds shut for another twenty-five years!) Nor does the term "mid-life" do us any good. Anne Mauch started negotiating the off-ramp at the ripe young age of thirty-nine, and in her case, it was not a moment too soon.

The discovery that life's too short and your job is too long can hit at any time — in early, mid, or late life. You needn't spend a decade or two in autopilot to know that you're wasting precious time, that you really ought to make your move. Colleagues and friends may tell you to stick with it, that work is hard, there's no free ride, you've got to pay your dues, etc. And no doubt they're right — to a point. But it's up to you to determine where that point is, and to make it a turning point. Caution is fine, but courage is better — and these days it requires courage to take your job in your hands and change it.

It requires courage to get to that elusive grail, *choice*. Most of us, most of the time, don't believe we have the privilege of choosing, yet we pine for it. Here's the irony: Of those who enjoy this privilege through wealth or who earn it through talent and hard work, few actually use it to increase their fortunes in life. Most of us simply get stuck, losing sight of the choices we might make — if not to stop working, then to change how we work, or at the very least, to change how we *think* about work. These are the choices that count, ultimately, because they empower us to know where we're going, and why. We can't always get there today, or next year. But we can plan — and watch for an opening to put that plan into action. This is the only remedy for the disease of inertia, which infects most of us. Not that we're all lying around doing nothing and feeling sorry for ourselves. We're busy, we're stretched to the limit, and we're doing the best that we can. But when we examine the results, we see that most of the time we're busy doing what we did yesterday, which prevents us from looking for what we might do differently tomorrow.

It wasn't easy getting myself unstuck. There were times when my mid-course correction was in grave danger of foundering into mid-life crisis, precipitated by changes in my husband's work that saw him taking frequent and extended business trips to Toronto. I often felt like a single working mom with an all-too-consuming job, and it was easy to fall into a funk of exhaustion and resentment. During the day, I'd nod off at managers' meetings. At night I'd weep over the laundry, then lie awake worrying about all the things I wouldn't have time to do the next day. What we needed to find was a way that two Type-A, career-driven people could rework their schedules and priorities to make time for a life. While Shaw's work was inherently inflexible, mine could be done in a variety of ways, including part-time, at home. I needed to invent a new model of success, and to do it I would have to quit my job.

I have a strong hunch that many women who say they don't want to work any more actually do — they just need a break, and the chance to put their working lives back together again in a healthier and more satisfying way. They don't want to be slaves to employers, or doormats to husbands and children. They want the permission — indeed, the right — to work in a way that sustains rather than destroys their lives, that leaves time for them to do essential work at home and in their communities. Increasingly, women (and more than a few family-oriented men) are demanding such things of their employers, and little by little they're being heard. The kind of work/life balance I have achieved at home is now achievable in many workplaces — and not only the ones where we're our own bosses. They're achievable at family-friendly companies where the staff is seen not just as payroll, but as people who want to live whole lives and who make better workers when allowed to do so.

ONE

Superwoman Grounded

Until very recently, *not* working scared the living daylights out of me. It's not that I was a workaholic. The wheelspinning, self-defeating perfectionism that defines textbook workaholism was never my vice. The workaholic's life is strung out along an ever-diminishing thread of meaning, where only work matters and everything — including work — suffers. I, on the other hand, favoured the multitasking model of life, where every single big or little thing you are called upon to do (by your boss, your staff, your partner, your parents, your children, their teachers, your friends, your personal trainer, your tax accountant, your cleaning lady, your cleaning lady's sister) is number one priority right this minute. And I always managed to fit it all in, with nanoseconds to spare. I was a one-woman military operation, not to mention a "well-balanced person." I derived a good deal of pride from all this. Men looked up to me. Women often asked, How do you do it?

As the years wore on, the demands increased and I became even more balanced, damn it. Always did my duty to company, family, community. Never missed a press deadline or failed to get home in time to toss a salad, calmly discuss the events of the day around the dinner table, oversee homework, read a bedtime story, update the grocery list, glance at the Daytimer, proof-read a couple of features, call

Mom, have a nice long soak in the tub, then curl up between snapping-clean sheets with an important new Canadian novel, followed by a round (or two!) of howling good sex.

Okay, so I lied about the last few items. Still, I did lead a rather impressive life — at least from the outside. On the inside, I was a wreck, systematically short-changing myself and, as a result, many of the people around me for years, possibly even decades, though I can't be certain exactly when the charade began, because large chunks of time (between 1980 and 1993) seem to have slipped through the cracks in my memory. I know for sure that during those thirteen-odd years, Shaw and I had two children, bought and sold three homes, traded several cars, and acquired a cottage and a boat and a six-figure credit line. I worked mostly for one company, where I climbed the ladder to find myself responsible for a monthly magazine read by a quarter of a million western Canadians. I had the privilege of working with a team of smart, good-hearted people, and enjoyed perks that extended to exotic vacations at prices only a magazine editor could afford. For all this, I counted myself extremely lucky. So lucky, in fact, that I dared not complain.

By the early '90s I had cultivated the appearance of a calm executive who'd happily reached her stride, while feeling more like a crazed carousel pony going up and down, round and round, faster and faster, about to come unpinned. I lost the ability to concentrate on a single task for more than ten minutes (a multitasker's occupational hazard). Amazingly, this did not create major problems at work, and might even have looked like a management strategy. But at home it felt like insanity. I cooked and ate in autopilot, one eye on the clock; my rope was only *this* long for homework help, and I would edit bedtime stories for brevity. I quit jogging in favour of violent spurts on the Stairmaster; I started looking my age, plus ten; I craved a vacation the day after I got back from one; while I always knew where my daughters were, I started to wonder *who* they were. And what about me? Who was I?

These are precisely the questions one avoids if one wants to remain a high-functioning member of the workforce. Once I started asking them, my life in the fast lane was as good as over. Oh, my body was still hurtling along, but my spirit had skidded to a halt. In fact, the whole internal landscape changed sometime towards the end of 1994. Instead of dreaming myself into the shoes of Martha Stewart or Marcia Clark, I wistfully watched my neighbour walk her kids to school. I devoured a book called *Your Money or Your Life*, and imagined myself broke but happy, living in a small town, doing (at most) one thing at a time: canning tomatoes, or knitting a sweater, or just sleeping — alone, on an army cot, because Shaw would surely have left me by then. Fortunately, I had the sense to keep these dreams to myself, quietly plotting the change that I knew was inevitable but might also prove disastrous if made rashly.

I don't think anyone at *Western Living* knew what I was thinking — or they wouldn't have been quite so stunned when I quit. But some of my friends knew, by intuition. I should point out that I have two groups of friends, the part-timers and the full-timers, and over the

> **I cooked and ate in autopilot, one eye on the clock; my rope was only *this* long for homework help, and I would edit bedtime stories for brevity.**

last twenty-odd years I have learned to dance from one to the other, depending on mood and schedule. They have indulged my needs, and I theirs, as old friends will. My best part-time-working friends are a writer, a social worker, and a therapist. They inhabit the camp where work is neatly and, for the most part, happily arranged around home and family. They get together often, usually over tea, children underfoot. All three have, at various times, castigated me for my months-long communication blackouts, but they have never made me feel unwelcome, should my schedule permit a cup-on-the-run.

My best full-time-working friends are an outspoken labour lawyer, a globe-trotting oncologist, and a celebrity businesswoman — a formidable trio. They also have kids, and husbands who tend to be artists. The full-timers get together less often than the part-timers, but with greater gusto, perhaps because of the necessity to blow off steam.

Every five or six weeks we convene a Girls' Night Out, always at some recently opened restaurant that has a costly menu and good wine list. Most of our fun is had at the expense of mutual friends — some of whom would like to join the group, but we would never let them because then whom would we talk about? Likewise, if one of us four "girls" ever misses a dinner date, it's open season on her. But the really heavy ammo is reserved for women who wear jogging pants and don't work.

Since I quit, Girls' Night Out tends to leave me with mild indigestion. At a recent one, in fact, I think I may have driven a wedge between my friends by mentioning how nice it was not to be working. One of the girls greeted that news with a loud toast and a confession that she, too, was tempted to trade in her Ferragamos for fuzzy slippers. Another seemed offended, somehow. The third wisely clammed up. For a few tense minutes, we eyed each other across an antipasto platter that had turned into the Rubicon.

These days, tea with the part-timers seems to go down a lot easier. Where I used to see them as sluglike in their professional drive, I now suspect they are as smart, liberated, and ambitious as my other friends, but a lot more sensible. They have simply traded in speed for sustainability, and accepted a degree of tedium in the bargain. Maybe I've known this all along, but never admitted it — which is why I felt their eyes burning holes in the back of my head when I returned to work after the briefest of maternity leaves, and when I soon afterwards weaned my first child in order to go on a business trip. They were the chorus of my conscience when I went from three to four days a week the following year, in order to take a promotion from staff writer to managing editor (promising myself at the same time that I'd never work five), and they nudged me again, eighteen months later, when I ate my promise and leapt to fill the empty shoes of editor-in-chief: full-time, plus nights and weekends. I cut my conscience off at the pass: how often do great jobs like this come up? How bad can it really be for my kids?

Our daughters (the younger one just out of diapers by then) didn't appear to be suffering so far, I told myself — at least not any more than the equally whiny and miserable kids of my stay-at-home friends. It's amazing how far one will stoop when ambition mixes with self-righteousness. I patted myself on the back for giving my girls the opportunity of day care, where they could get a leg up on early socialization — using "words instead of fists," playing dress-up drama, building block forts, and eating kiwi fruit served by calm (salaried) caregivers — while stay-at-home kids were watching *Sesame Street* on a six-hour VCR loop and munching Oreos tossed to them by frazzled (unsalaried) moms.

This sort of thinking kept me up and running at work, but at home, late at night, self-righteousness dissolved into a slough of doubt. Fatigue ate away at my defences; I shuddered at the prospect of leaving for work the next morning, and the next, and the next, with my younger daughter clinging, crying, begging me to stay home. Fortunately, most nights, I was able to sleep off my doubts and wake up with fresh resolve. Anyway, she got over it within a year or two, by which time we had taken both girls out of day care (socialization be damned) and hired a nanny — a practical if expensive decision, crowned by the good fortune of finding an enormously capable woman whom our children adored and who stayed with us for several years.

This was more like it: coming home to happy children and a clean house, dinner roasting in the oven, cats fed, mail sorted, garbage out. I promised myself always to have a baby either at home or on the way, to ensure that I could always have a nanny. It was during this time that Shaw and I purchased the cottage — quality time would be ours, if we could squeeze it in! We also moved from a handyman special to a large new house, furnishing it to *Western Living* standards, on the strength of our credit line.

Then, around the time our daughters were approaching the pre-teen years, we had a childcare crisis. Or more accurately, *I* had a childcare crisis, precipitated by a steep increase in Shaw's business travel — his company opened a Toronto office and put him in charge. A good part of the time, I was thrust into the role of single mom, but without the perks — such as the freedom to find a new husband who'd *be there* when I needed him. To make matters worse, we were phasing out the nanny — not because she was incapable of minding our children for fifty-odd hours a week (she no doubt was). But "minding" no longer seemed adequate for the kids, and her salary no longer commensurate with the challenge — the colossal feats of patience and loving coercion required to get a peevish eight-year-old to practise the piano, for example, or to get a ten-year-old to read the book before writing the report. I know our nanny could have, and would have, done these things. She would have provided the shoulder to cry on when young friendships crashed and burned, and had her antennae up for red-alert peer pressure. With the help of strict guidelines, a cell phone, and danger pay, she might have been armed to "babysit" kids who didn't really think they needed watching but who didn't mind having someone cook and clean up for them. She might have done all that, but the truth is I didn't want her to. I wanted to be the primary caregiver, the guide, the disciplinarian, the role model, the bitch — whatever was called for.

> **Once you arrive at superwoman status, it is very hard to renounce the role and accept the blame for the stress and misery it can bring.**

But I was busy working most of the time. What was I to do? This was not a unique problem, not by a long shot. Walk into any large office and you can quickly identify that subset of working women who have teenage kids at home. Look for the premature strands of grey, the cover-up-defying frown lines, and the ticlike response to phones or pagers going off, especially between the hours of 3:00 and 6:00. The hard-core subset of working mothers of teens are the single working moms of teens, and if you're looking for a course in survival skills, let these women be your teachers. But don't even think about bringing a working dad into the loop, particularly if he's your boss.

Which brings me to the Virtually Single Male, or VSM, a very large subset of working men. Your boss is probably one of these, as mine have always been. The higher you go on the corporate ladder, the more VSM-dominated life becomes. The framed photos on a VSM's desk may indicate that he has a spouse and children, but you must not assume he is interested in them, or in yours, between the hours of 8:00 and 6:00. Nor do these framed faces pose any serious obstacle to after-hours bar visits (so important to staff morale) or to impromptu business trips. In communicating with a VSM, the working mother must guard against undue honesty. When he breaks the ice before your annual performance appraisal with a question like, "So how's the new baby?" your answer should be: "Great. Just great. Now, how about those third-quarter results, eh?" The VSM is interested only in your undivided attention to the task, or to him, or both. That's why he's the boss. In his presence, and in any bar or restaurant within a two-kilometre radius, you are obliged to don the mantle of a ladder-climbing VSF (Virtually Single Female). Either that, or take the nearest snake down, and out.

I did my share of VSF role-playing, and even came to see it as the necessary lie that guarantees some business gets done in floor space leased at office rates. Plenty of women would rail against such an attitude, arguing that the workplace has to change to reflect the real needs of parents and children in today's society — that it should not be necessary to sneak out to the fire escape just to talk about your kids. And they're right. The pace set by Virtually Single Males skews the odds against ambitious women. The high-functioning VSM has a wife at home taking care of all those pesky, time-consuming household matters, from sorting out their kids' lives to separating his socks. With a support system like that in place, and a similar one at the office (where an executive assistant sorts out his life and separates his faxes), the senior VSM is not actually living a lie. He doesn't have to. His working day wouldn't be a whole lot different if he were single. Not so the VSF, who must sort out her own life, her kids' lives, *and* her husband's socks.

In a better world, women would be proud of all they accomplished, and wouldn't need to play charades. In an even better world, men would share those accomplishments and that pride. Unfortunately, most of us live and work in the real world, where honesty must be handled with care. So I discreetly made the rounds in our office, gleaning what I could from other post-nanny, post-day-care moms who were miraculously functional at work and whose children were still, by all accounts, alive.

A common strategy, I found, was to keep your kids so busy, bouncing from one after-school activity to another, that you never had to worry about what they were (or weren't) doing. I tried this for a year or so. I lived, breathed, and slept car-pools. I was on the phone morning, noon, and night, when I wasn't in the car, which had turned into the dining room. At work I became an obsessive clock-watcher, as the pressure mounted to leave at exactly 5:02 on Mondays, Wednesdays, and Fridays, 5:11 on Tuesdays, and 4:58 on Thursdays — failure to do so resulting in a curbside riot of damp, shivering kids arguing over whose useless mom was supposed to be picking them up. And the really maddening thing was, the kids didn't appreciate spending all those productive and expensive hours skating, singing in choirs, tap dancing, and learning to Build With Clay. "Why can't I just come home after school today?" one or the other would often ask at breakfast. Sometimes I relented: "Okay, but don't open the door to strangers, don't watch TV, and don't eat junk. Oh, and practise the piano."

Next, I tried flex hours — an early shift that would allow me to be home when my kids got home from school. And so began a two-year blur of activity that must have taken me through my fortieth birthday, because I have snapshots to that effect. My routine consisted of getting up at 5:45 to be at the office by 7:00, then racing through the day to justify what my 9:00-to-5:00 staff considered an early exit at 3:00, which often stretched to 4:00 out of guilt. Then came the reward — that precious before-dinner hiatus that could be used in dozens of productive ways, and always was. It was at this time that I perfected my multitasking method of being all things to all people, including myself. One or two whole hours in the middle of the day was a glorious gift of time, an unprecedented luxury not to be taken lightly, so I proceeded to pack them full to bursting with quality bytes: housework was done quickly to make room for hobbies and sports of choice for the girls, workouts for me, and piano lessons all around. I even signed up for a sushi-rolling class.

On good days I was still vertical, even cheerful, when Shaw arrived home at 7:00, which is not to say I was alert enough to have an adult conversation. Mercifully, he humoured me and kept a safe distance, confident that I would eventually wake up and crave his company again, maybe even before he turned sixty-five. On bad days, I found myself still wide awake at midnight, sorting laundry and kicking myself for missing an important managers' meeting that had been called for 4:30 or, worse, for skipping the latest Girls' Night Out because I was too beat. Ears burning, legs aching, I hurled myself into the bed that I had made and would have to sleep in.

If you're thinking I'm my own worst enemy, and that somebody ought to have given me a good shake, you'd be partially right. I was not being sensible, as my mother would say (and often did). A sensible person would ease up on the demands: let the laundry pile up, let the kids roll with the punches, simply let up at work. But have I ever characterized myself as a sensible person? I am a maniac: a hardcore Type-A worker, homemaker, *and* mom, which is a deadly combination and — here's the scary part — no mere personal quirk. It's the genetic make-up of all the so-called superwomen you see dashing through boardrooms, leaping gazelle-like in aerobics classes, and wearing pagers to Christmas pageants. Just try giving us all a shake; we'll shake you right back. Strength in numbers! And strength in status, of which we get way too much. We are held up as role models, and thus the mania feeds itself. Once you arrive at superwoman status, it is very hard to renounce the role and accept the blame for the stress and misery it can bring. It's much easier to blame someone else. Like your husband. Or your mother.

Was my mom guilty, for raising me in boom times and with the boom notion of the world being my oyster? Well, that was hardly her fault. Her generation wanted it all for us, their daughters, and why not? Equality was an idea they were just reading about when we arrived on the scene, able and willing to breathe life into it. We wouldn't have to make the tough choices they did: family or career? Husband or self? Didn't Betty Friedan say it was time to smash the old wife/mother image — the stifling "feminine mystique" that says women "can find fulfillment only in sexual passivity, male domination, and nurturing maternal love"? Yes, she did, but she said it twenty years after quitting a doctoral program in psychology to get married, have kids, and stay home. You could say Betty Friedan had it all, but never all at the same time.

In fairness, my mother did know best, and was quite clear about the kind of careers she thought her three daughters should have: the kind you can "fall back on." First things first went without saying: make a home, raise children, change the world. A lot of women I know accepted this as the proper order of things. These are not necessarily "traditional" women. Nor is wealth a key factor, though a few are wealthy enough to consider the second income a luxury rather than a necessity. Most could have put that income to good use, but chose to forgo it. A friend once expressed this to me in terms I'll never forget. "Sometimes I think I should go back to work," she said. "But then I think, do I really need a new sofa?"

What she said hurt me, and not only because I had recently purchased a nice new sofa, which she knew, and I knew she knew. It hurt because it forced me to examine my values, for the hundredth time that week. I had an interesting job, but was I changing the world, and if not, was it worth it? Certainly Shaw and I could survive on one income — sell the house, the sofa, whatever — and I could put some real energy into bringing a pulse back into my home. Make it the kind of home I grew up in, instead of a nicely furnished pit where speeding bodies stop for fuel and sleep.

A pulse is not something you can fake. You can try to, but your family will see right through it, and hate you for it. This, more or less, was the conclusion of a study published by the New York–based Families and Work Institute. In a broad workplace survey, researchers found that children (between six and eighteen) were resigned to the fact that their parents worked, but they were plenty mad at having to cope with the resulting bad moods. When asked, "If you could do one thing to improve family life, what would it be?" most of the kids surveyed did not give the expected answer: more time with their parents. They did say they'd like their parents to come home "less wired, less in a bad mood, less keyed up, less tired."

Yeah, right. We all know this, but how do we do it? My part-time-working friends would say: choose. But there's an easy answer, according to the self-help industry. You can have it all, so long as you "balance" it. It's no surprise that this

I was going to quit my job and gain control of my personal life. I didn't yet know exactly how I would swing this, but swing it I must . . .

industry has boomed over the last decade, especially the niche devoted to helping the working woman help herself. An American company called CareerTrack pitched a one-day course to our office last year. It was titled "Life Balance Workshop for Working Women: How to be on top of your job and in control of your personal life." For about thirty seconds, I considered taking it.

The CareerTrack brochure, which was posted on the bulletin board in our lunch room, showed a gracefully running woman with hair flying, arms and legs in balletic leaping position, a set of scales in one hand. "Put an end to the misguided beliefs that keep you running ragged," blared the caption. I opened the brochure and quickly found myself both exhausted and demoralized by the twenty-one-point curriculum. In six hours, CareerTrack promised to teach me to define priorities, make necessary trade-offs ("without self-defeating inner conflict"), establish support systems, and make time for myself. I would learn ways to start each day with a "clearly defined sense of purpose," find out when to be there for others and when to push my do-not-disturb button, how to set limits my family and boss would respect — in short, how to organize myself for "peak efficiency at work and at home." The price of the workshop was $99 — money well spent (said CareerTrack) by employers who wished to see their female employees come running back all balanced and happy and raring to work harder than ever.

Nothing on a bulletin board is sacred, especially at a magazine office. Every typo gets circled, every face gets a moustache, every want ad gets answered by a phantom pervert, every brochure gets rewritten. I rewrote this one, with the headline: "De-Motivational Workshop for Working Women: How to quit your job and gain control of your personal life." Instead of stress control, my curriculum focused on anger release; in place of balancing, binge eating. Three hours, mid-afternoon, was given over to a nap.

I posted my brochure, then tore it down, realizing in the nick of time that it wasn't funny. Coming from a manager, it was incendiary, not to mention insulting — to all the women in my office who didn't have the option of quitting, or the desire to do so. But the exercise was somehow therapeutic for me, clinching a decision I had already made but hadn't faced. I was going to quit my job and gain control of my personal life. I didn't yet know exactly how I would swing this, but swing it I must, or lose my mind.

It took weeks to make a plan, and months more to gather support from my family to implement it. The plan involved moving to the suburbs, where the equity from our city house would buy us a perfectly nice replacement, mortgage-free or close to it. We would sell the cottage, or find partners, thus reducing debt to the point that my physical presence, rather than my executive salary, would become my major contribution to the household for the next five years or so. Oh, I would still have to bring in some money, according to my calculations. Life on one salary was simply not in the cards, though one-and-a-half would see us through our monthly stack of bills. The stack would be smaller, in any case, without my $160 shoes and $50 haircuts — and maybe if we shopped at Costco we could still afford to go out for sushi on Saturday nights.

Earning half an income should not be all that hard, I thought. I would set up an office at home, like everyone else I knew, and on the isolated occasions when I found myself there, I would write articles. This would prevent total professional eclipse — something that worried me more than the modest material sacrifices in my plan. A budget haircut I could live with, but invisibility? I knew myself too well to believe I'd be content falling off the face of the earth, which is what home-making looks like to the non-homemaker. And anyway, a cold quit would make it impossible to get back into the professional loop when the kids are older and I'm ready. Rusty skills and an out-of-date Rolodex would be no help at all.

Once I had my plan in place, I slept easy. Not so my family. Shaw wasn't thrilled about moving downmarket, having spent so many years moving up. The kids were justifiably upset about leaving neighbourhood friends. All three were jangled about losing the cottage, their favourite place in the world. Only I was remarkably calm, right up to and through my notice period. For the first time in decades, I was focusing on one thing. Change.

And change we did. We found a charming house at the right price in a pleasant suburban neighbourhood, close to good schools; we found excellent cottage partners in my sister and her family; we semi-retired the mortgage and watched the credit line crash.

Between the writing of the article and the release of this book, my universe fell apart and came back together again in a sometimes painful but always interesting way. For the first time in my adult life, I was able to get far enough away from the nine-to-five world to actually start missing many things about it, and to understand why most people want to be there. There were days when I would have liked to be there, too. Staying home presents its own steep challenges: Whether you are there to raise children or write a book or run a home-based business, there is plenty of work to be done, and precious few people around to support your efforts, keep you on task, buy you lunch. But don't get me wrong — I'm not complaining. Most days I appreciate that what I bargained for is a rare luxury

— the time and space to decompress, to reclaim my deepest desires, and, I hope, to figure out a way to make all this pay so that Shaw might have the chance to do the same thing before he hits sixty-five.

The first challenge was simply to slow down. In my first few months at home, I whirled about like a domestic dervish. I couldn't drive past a supermarket without stopping to pick up something. I made a pest of myself at my younger daughter's school, sitting at the back of the class, taking notes. At home, I piled hobby on hobby, chore on chore: cranking up the stereo while baking pies, sewing cushion covers, answering e-mail, cleaning the drip pan under the fridge — there's a drip pan under my fridge! I reported all this to my family and they humoured me, knowing it would pass.

> **For the first time in my adult life, I was able to get far enough away from the nine-to-five world to actually start missing many things about it . . .**

And it did pass, some time around the fourth month. Oh yes, it did. Somnambulism is one way to describe the next stage of my decompression. If I were a wintering mole, I couldn't have been more dormant. I moved slowly, thought slowly, read slowly, went to bed early and slept late. My taste in music turned to operas, and I would lie on the couch and listen from start to finish, then go back to the really mushy arias and weep, thinking of my late dad who used to sing along. I'd walk the dog till we were both dizzy and weak, then get home in time to supervise the making of dinner, from the couch. Looking back, I suppose I was depressed, but having never experienced such a thing before, I had no label for this lack of focus, this motivational drought. It was something I had to go through, like the long sleep after a fever breaks.

I think I snapped out of it the day my thirteen-year-old daughter burst into the house in her usual after-school exuberance, then froze as though she'd seen a ghost. And I guess she had — an apparition in rubber gloves, sweat dripping from its nose, a black smudge across one eye. I was feeling energetic that day and was washing the windows. Her look told me she was appalled. It doesn't take much for a girl that age to be appalled, especially by her mother, and I thought I was well defended against taking such things personally. But something in that look gave me a start. Who does she see when she looks at me? Who *am* I?

The irony is laughable. Here I'd come home to my nest, in large part to get to know my family better, and what happened? I lost sight of myself. The window-washing moment jump-started a new line of questioning which led, in turn, to a new line of thinking — about work, and identity, and the way we put those things together. I realized that the challenge ahead of me, from that point, was to find a comfort zone large enough to accommodate all the different kinds of work I wanted to do — for love, for money, *and* for a better view of the trees through smudgy windows.

In the months that followed, I started writing again, in earnest, from my little office at the back of the house. I imposed a nine-to-five schedule on myself, taking a quick break for lunch and a longer one after school to accommodate the girls' schedules. I tried not to consider the late-afternoon hours stolen from me if (when) they were consumed by car pools, dentist visits, and the like. I gave those hours up freely, and made them up later — at night or on weekends when Shaw was doing family duty. With my old energy and resolve having returned in spades, I had no problem finding ways to get my work done, and soon enough went looking for more. I landed a short-term lectureship in the publishing program at Simon Fraser University, and discovered that I loved to teach. I offered to run a writing workshop for our district's high-school enrichment program, and was thrilled when they took me up on it. But mostly I stayed home and wrote, heeding my twin callings: motherhood and the muse.

CHECK |
Your Timetable

THE TWELVE-WEEK COUNTDOWN TO QUITTING

I gave my boss three months' notice before quitting. I viewed this as a common courtesy — a way to make a gracious exit from a good, long-term job. It would allow my employer and me to work together on finding a replacement, but more importantly (from my selfish perspective) it would set a timetable that was just long enough, but not too long, for my own thorny transition from employee to ex-employee.

This "countdown" is more playful than practical, but it does reflect a few universal truths about leaving a job. For instance: your responsibility to your successor, the imperative to make a real break from the old work before leaping into the new, the resistance (even fatigue) you will feel on facing the challenge of reinventing yourself, and the unique mixture of joy and dread that will colour the whole transition. Ready? Start counting.

Week One

DO: give notice
DON'T: spread the word until your boss has
EXPECT: to feel relief mingled with regret
TIP: breathe

Week Two

DO: keep your head down
DON'T: gloat
EXPECT: to feel the urge to call in sick
TIP: don't

Week Three

DO: prepare for the news to get around

DON'T: assume they'll be happy for you
EXPECT: to field questions
TIP: keep answers short

Week Four

DO: offer to help with succession
DON'T: let on you don't care
EXPECT: to feel like a hypocrite
TIP: practise sincerity in front of a mirror

Week Five

DO: start focusing on transition
DON'T: neglect your work
EXPECT: to feel stretched, stressed
TIP: take long baths

Week Six

DO: reconnect with the outside world
DON'T: do this only for professional gain
EXPECT: to feel isolated by colleagues
TIP: make a souvenir scrapbook

Week Seven

DO: review reasons for leaving
DON'T: give in to halfway regret
EXPECT: inertia, fatigue
TIP: keep working on that scrapbook

Week Eight

DO: update your résumé
DON'T: send it out to three hundred employers
EXPECT: periods of panic
TIP: get lost in a novel

Week Nine

DO: bring your novel to work

DON'T: hesitate to read it

EXPECT: to feel like a freeloader

TIP: try to stay awake

Week Ten

DO: spring cleaning

DON'T: throw away anything useful

EXPECT: the urge to jeopardize your successor

TIP: resist

Week Eleven

DO: shop for goodbye gifts

DON'T: leave unnecessary work for others

EXPECT: to feel like crying

TIP: go ahead

Week Twelve

DO: be gracious, honest

DON'T: expect to get any work done

EXPECT: see week one

TIP: take the rest of the day off

TWO

The New Meaning of Work

THAT WAS THEN	THIS IS NOW
Livelihood	Life
Compensation	Reward
Excellence	Turbulence
Profits	Prophets
Grey flannel suit	Plaid flannel shirt
Slavery	Poetry
Keep up the pace	Put it on pause
Job	Work
Freedom 55	Freedom now
Going for speed	Going for depth
Fear	Courage
Fast track	Winding road
Success	Satisfaction
Hierarchy	Web
Survival	Growth

Our first challenge is to take a hard look at the notion of working. What does work *mean?* What's a *job?* And, more specifically, how is it that so many of us experience "working" and "living" as parallel worlds, each with its own language, value system, and daily rhythms?

We're one person at work, another at home. We "leave work" where it is best left: at the office. At least, that's what we do when we are considered well-adjusted. To those sorry souls who bring their work home with them, we say: Get a life!

It is precisely this notion of work that is worth leaving, and the sooner the better. Work need not inhabit a world apart from life — indeed, the natural way to approach work is precisely the way you would approach the things that bring the most satisfaction in life. Take *live* out of livelihood and all you've got is a job. Interesting that *Webster's* dictionary includes an obsolete definition of the word livelihood: "the quality or state of being lively." When did this become obsolete? Was it around the same time that "compensation" came to be used as a synonym for wages — when work became so bad for us that we had to be paid damages?

This is an implicit deal we make in the workplace: we receive more money for our willingness to be hamstrung by office politics, bullied by bureaucracies. As the rewards go up, the fun diminishes — which may explain why we call executive salaries "serious money." But even the best-paid executives are beginning to see that work need not be so punishing. Why, after all, should our work not draw from that same wellspring of passion, energy, and creativity that informs our favourite pastimes? Because that's life in the latter half of the twentieth century, you say? Because you have no choice? Because you're lucky to have a job, even if it's *just a job,* when millions are losing theirs? Or worse: Because you *have no pastimes?*

A growing number of people are seeing in these last years of the millennium a unique opportunity to rethink the way they live *and* work. Rethinking doesn't necessarily entail quitting anything — though it did for me. Mostly it entails questioning whether we've been spending a lot of valuable time "making a living," or have in fact been busy making a dying. That's what happens when there is no reward for working other than working itself; when, as Gertrude Stein put it, you realize there's no *there,* there; when you notice that work has begun to feed itself, is growing bigger and greedier, and the most important things in your life — the *real* work of loving, learning, sharing, and growing — are being squeezed right out of the picture.

PUTTING WORK ON PAUSE

When we're working, and especially when we're doing double duty at home and in the office, it's hard to stop and take stock. We tend to shift into autopilot. We put our heads down and keep flying — organizing the clutter of our work and home lives into twin piles, in-tray for work, out-tray for home. The neatness of the piles is reassuring until, all of a sudden, we hit an air pocket. Perhaps a co-worker is fired without warning. Or a family member falls ill. We go in for the crash landing and all that neatly stacked paper hits the fan; our two separate worlds collide and chaos reigns.

This is not as bad for us as it sounds. As modern science has amply demonstrated, the fundamental organizing principle of the universe is chaos. Now, we have joined it. With a bit of creativity and more than a little courage, we'll be able to apply some organizing principles to ourselves and emerge the better for it. We've been forced to stop, take stock, and reset our compass.

> **A growing number of people are seeing these last years of the millennium as a unique opportunity to rethink the way they live *and* work.**

Though the free fall of chaos is a frightening state to be in, it's reassuring to discover yourself going down in very good company. Everything seems to be in flux these days, especially in the world of work. This is something you will not likely notice, of course, until you *stop* working. At your job, it's the same old routine, day after day, with customers to serve, quotas to meet, profit-and-loss statements and performance appraisals to worry about, bonuses to hope for, goals to set and meet and set again. There's an uncanny order to it all and, too often, a terrible tedium. There is also a lulling sense of security in simply doing the same things over and over, especially when you are surrounded by co-workers all doing the *same* same things. The occasional glimpse outside your workplace windows reveals not freedom but mayhem — and so you yank the blinds shut. You put your head back down.

The mayhem is no illusion, your deepest fears not groundless. It *is* a jungle out there — a madhouse of conflicting values and priorities that's thrown business leaders and politicians into a muddle over the past few years. There are no clear directives from either the right or the left, and with so many shrill voices gathering in the centre, it's hard to hear yourself think. Is the economy declining, or is it rebounding? Is joblessness (even homelessness) something I should worry about for myself? For my children? Or is that hysteria? Can I trust my human resources department, and if not, whom can I talk to? The guy at the next desk? What if he's after my job?

Insecurity has become a way of life for countless North Americans — those who have lost jobs, and those who fear losing them. Predictably, the reassurance business is booming. Everywhere we turn, business gurus and media experts reassure us that we're fine, we can take charge of our lives if we just buy this book or listen to that tape. Where a few years ago the bookstore Ph.D.s were selling excellence, now they've switched to spirituality, which is much more reassuring (if a bit vague on the remuneration side). Prophets instead of profits — get yours today! The man in the grey flannel suit has morphed into the guy in the plaid flannel shirt. Pop Buddhism is booming, and so is Simplicity — the movement, not the sewing company. What started in the late 1980s as a threadbare cadre of Seattle coffee-shop regulars with too much time on their hands has mushroomed into a righteous army of downshifting boomers, dedicated to nailing shut the lid on materialism's coffin. Their very presence screams this challenge: What are all you people killing yourselves for? The old reward system is dead. Get over it!

Such attitudes are no longer relegated to the "alternative" fringe. Indeed, alternative has gone mainstream. The business pages of even the most conservative newspapers are filled with radical advice. "Organizational world is changing before our very eyes," shouts a headline in *The Globe and Mail*'s "Working Issues" quarterly, followed by this advice:

> You add to what you know, you adjust what you do. Constantly. No matter what sector you work in, no matter at what level, no matter under what contract, go immediately to the mirror and greet your self-manager. That title means you are finally now in charge of the last enterprise on Earth you will always be able to keep working for.

Yes, this sounds reassuring, but what exactly does it mean? That we're only as secure as we feel on gazing at our reflections in the mirror? What if I don't have a self-management bone in my body? Whatever happened to company loyalty that went both ways — employees who wanted to take company goals personally, and employers who could be trusted to safeguard the interests of their staff? If the media is to be believed, all that is dust in the wind.

Of course nothing is ever as bleak as the media might suggest. Plenty of employers have weathered the downsizing wars and emerged more caring than callous towards their people. But there is no denying that the work world has been radically altered from the one our parents knew and from the one we set our sights on as we beavered through school and job training. Even those fortunate employees working for liberated companies are obliged to rethink their long-term goals and priorities. Everyone has been touched, to some degree, by the chaos of the times, and the result is that there's more sifting and sorting going on than you'll find in a candy factory. Everyone is trying to figure out whether we're living in the best of times or the worst of times, whether we're going forward or backward.

The only way to figure that out for yourself is to put your work life on pause — if not for a year, then for a moment — and indulge in the art of wondering, of returning to that stage of early adulthood before reality first slashed through the arc of possibility. We can call this chaos, or we can call it liberation, which is less frightening and therefore more useful. By joining the wonderers, we depart that rigid place in which our jobs, and how we do them, is prescribed. Indeed, we can get away from the world that wants to call us by our jobs. She's a lawyer; he's a bank manager, they're "just" secretaries. Right now, in this time of great flux, nothing is prescribed. Now is our chance to get unstuck: to do something radical, for a change — *if only for a change.*

IN THE COMPANY OF QUITTERS

One of the things I've made time for, by putting my "day job" on pause, is browsing the Internet — connecting with an international community of wonderers and virtual wanderers. My initial motivation in getting wired was to become, as one business magazine puts it, "cybersavvy." I figured this would be an essential tool in my reworking kit. A way to think global and act global, as it were. And maybe it will pay off one day in professional connections — who knows? But the immediate reward has been social, which is probably what I was truly looking for in my early stages of at-home isolation.

> Browsing the Internet— the immediate reward has been social, which is probably what I was truly looking for in my early stages of at-home isolation.

It has been an eye-opening experience. The info highway is clogged with browsers, all blinking the sleep of inertia out of their eyes, looking for answers to questions they'd never have thought to ask a few years ago. One of my first net hang-outs was *Cafe Utne*, the interactive/ electronic counterpart to the *Utne Reader* magazine. Two months after my quitting story was published here in Canada, that magazine ran a whole section titled "Just Quit! The Fine Art of Breaking Free," which lit up *Cafe Utne*'s wires for several ensuing weeks as readers logged on with quit-related thoughts, rants, and obsessions. I logged on, too, and found myself in very interesting company.

Cafe Utne's forum on quitting was remarkable for its vehemence and variety of response. Initial postings — the first thirty or forty — tended to celebrate the art of the quit. Their logic, in a nutshell, was this: Our jobs are among the few things we can control in a culture that hoards power far away from us. Trapped in a bad one? Just quit! Which is precisely what many of these *Cafe* visitors had done, it appeared. And done repeatedly. I guessed most of them were still young (you can spot Gen-Xers by the wired jargon, the aversion to paragraph breaks, and the lack of capital letters). The older crowd, by contrast, ambled into the *Cafe* later, with post after post inflamed by the fire and brimstone of experience: "All yang and no yin," offered one critic of the easy quit. Another — a woman who'd spent thirty-odd years essentially exploring her options in a succession of publishing internships — confessed now to a hunger for commitment.

> The constant change in itself becomes tedium. That's when it's time to quit quitting — when this *quitting* or exploring no longer feels fresh, exciting, broadening; when it's ceased to be a perpetual learning experience and is nothing but another unfulfilling routine. At that point, *sticktoitiveness* becomes the novelty…. And that's growth too, as long as it's undertaken with sincerity.

Then a *Cafe* regular named Bryan piped up with an elegant summary, suggesting that to lump all quitters together is folly. In fact, Bryan argued, there are three different kinds: the "socially challenged," who are happier on society's fringes; the "drifters," for whom a serious commitment is only a brief interlude between changes; and the "soul searchers," those who, at some point in their lives, "realize a crisis or crux of values and meaning, such that the course or content of their lives up to that point seem in retrospect to be nugatory or even destructive. These are the true quitters," wrote Bryan. "Those who have committed, tried, succeeded, or failed, and have to search their souls for an answer to the right thing to do. Can the term *quit* have any real meaning without prior commitment?"

Armed with my *Webster's* (nugatory *adj*: of little or no consequence), I joined the fray, riffing not on the word *quit,* but on the word *just*. "There's no point quitting a job *just* because you want to quit, then turning around and getting another job *just* because you still need to work," my posting began. It continued:

> Too many *just*s for my money. This is one thing that rattled me about the *UR* story, much as I enjoyed reading it. *Just* quit implies a certain impetuosity that's really quite absurd. Just eat a piece of fudge? No problem. But just quit? I feel the same way about the Nike ads. I mean, give me a break. If I *just did it* like the athletes in those ads, I'd never walk again. Ditto quitting. *Just* quit implies that it's too much bother to figure out how or why you ought to do this, so *just* go ahead and do it anyway. Wrong. Figuring out that stuff is what quitting is all about, at least to me. And it makes working look like a picnic. I found the hardest part was figuring out exactly what it was about my (enviable) job that wasn't working for me, and how I could apply that knowledge to the business of getting on with a productive and happier life — including the kind of work I'd be able to apply myself to in an energized and sustained fashion for a good, long period of time (because that's what it takes to do good work). This done, I wouldn't have to quit again in the near future, which would be a relief!

I got some meaty responses from my posting, including a note from a woman who was at that very time puzzling through the process of quitting her job, and through the whole thorny issue of what work meant to her.

> We've created this phenomenon of *work* as separate from the rest of our lives — most of us no longer directly produce what we need to live. Coupled with that is this phenomenon of *leisure* we've created that has evolved like nothing our fore-

bears would recognize. And coupled with all of that, we've created these ways of communicating and sending ourselves (travelling) across space and time and distances never before dreamed of. And I would argue that the more you open up the world, the more you learn, the more you are "dissatisfied" with settling — settling for what most careers currently demand — which is that you turn off your brain and any other aspect of yourself that is not your *job* self. When I start to think like this, half of me reprimands myself for being a spoiled child. Having the gall to think that *work* should be rewarding and fulfilling and challenging, and maybe sometimes even fun — with room for the other parts of you. Yet maybe I'm not alone."

No, maybe not. The postings kept right on coming from puzzled people across the continent — obviously, the magazine had struck a chord. *UR* editor Hugh Delehanty posted his pleasure.

My God, what have we wrought with this Just Quit section? Ever since the issue hit the stand, I've been deluged by friends and readers confessing their quitting dream wishes. My favourite was a poet friend who revealed his secret longing to stop writing about turning fifty. Three years ago he crossed the half-century mark, and he's still writing about it, poem after poem ad nauseam. He felt enslaved by the poems. They were strangling his creativity, not to mention his relationship with his wife. To someone else, writing poetry would be a source of liberation; to him, it had become a lonely psychic prison. Perhaps, inspired by the Just Quit issue, he will take the famous Lawrencian leap and get a new job as, say, a gerontologist.

In the chaos of our times, one enslaved poet struggles to be free of the muse, while thousands of working stiffs reach for the freedom of poetry.

Ten years ago
I turned my face for a moment
and it became my life.

This snippet of poetry is taken from *The Heart Aroused: Poetry and the Preservation of the Soul in Corporate America* by David Whyte, an English poet turned consultant whose business is booming in these soul-searching times. The quote is not actually Whyte's, but from a poem written by a woman who participated in one of his AT&T management seminars. Whyte's thrust, in the seminars and in his book, is to put soul back into work by rekindling our creative spark and rediscovering our passions. The first step is simply to pause.

"We were looking at the way human beings find it necessary to sacrifice their own sacred desires and personal visions on the altar of work and success," says Whyte, describing the theme of the seminar where the AT&T poet emerged. He goes on:

We have patience for everything but what is most important to us. We look at the life of our own most central imaginings and see it beckon. For the most part, we have not the courage to follow it, but we do not have the courage to leave it. We turn our face for a moment and tell ourselves we will be sure to get back to it. When we look again, ten years have passed and we wonder what in God's name happened to us.[*]

TOWARDS A WORKING-LESS WORLD

What *did* happen to us? All this angst about working and these dreams about quitting stem from the same seed of disappointment — in how things have turned out as opposed to how we thought they would. The world our parents delivered us into should have been in the palms of our hands by now. Labour-saving machines should be

---

[*]Reprinted from *The Heart Aroused*, by David Whyte; by permission of Doubleday, a division of Bantam Doubleday Dell Publishing Group, Inc.

doing the overtime work, freeing us up for better things than the daily dawn-to-dusk ordeal of trying (and often failing) to make ends meet. We should have more time for family and leisure — that's what the futurists promised us just a few decades ago. Instead we've become a nation divided, between the overworked, who can't find time for leisure, and the underworked, who can't afford it.

Statistics Canada surveys tell the story. Though the average employed adult works a forty-hour week, the reality is that the current crop of workers comprises fewer "average" employees than any of the past several generations. Today, most workers fall on either end of the scale: those who work substantially more than forty hours a week (including white-collar middle managers, professionals, and unionized labourers) and those who work far fewer (including clerical, self-employed, and non-union workers). Our downshifted economy is the main culprit, driving many companies to cut losses by working their highly skilled employees longer and hiring temporary or part-time staff to fill the gaps. This can bring a windfall of savings on payroll taxes and worker benefits, even with overtime payments factored in. It is easy for employers to justify such strategies, pointing to the fat pay cheques of those clocking overtime. But while some workers are no doubt pleased to pocket the extra cash, increasing numbers report a serious deficit on the satisfaction side of the ledger. A Statistics Canada study of 15,000 working Canadians found that almost one-third would be happy to work less for less pay.

> **Our downshifted economy is the main culprit, driving many companies to cut losses by working their highly skilled employees longer . . .**

A successful experiment at a Chrysler minivan plant in Windsor, Ontario, suggests a way to correct this imbalance. In 1993, the auto workers, backed by the Ontario Federation of Labour, refused to continue working overtime. They successfully negotiated with management to hire a third shift of permanent weekend workers — for a net gain of a thousand new jobs at the Chrysler plant. Results like this fuel the drive for change being spearheaded by progressive labour groups, economists, and politicians across the continent. In the United States, a prominent group of social activists (economists Jeremy Rifkin and Juliet Schor, Senator Eugene McCarthy, and pioneer feminist Betty Friedan among them) have joined forces with representatives of labour, women's support networks, and work/family advocates to hammer out some solutions to what they call "the North American time famine." In the spring of 1996, at the University of Iowa, the Shorter Work Time movement was launched, along with a manifesto that has come to be known as the *Iowa City Declaration*. Its leading recommendation states:

> We North Americans, gathered in Iowa City, therefore urge the national governments of Canada and the United States to put in place before the year 2000 the legal arrangements to ensure that a 32-hour workweek will become the norm for full-time workers in the first decade of the new millennium. While a reduced workweek is the focus of this appeal, we also recognize that longer vacations, sabbaticals, job-sharing, and other forms of hours reductions or alternative schedules are desirable objects. In the process of reducing work hours, it is important to protect and enhance the basic wage and benefit structure for workers in advanced economies, including those employed as part-time, contingent, temporary, or contract workers. We invite support for those objectives from representatives of the labor movement, the business community, public officials, religiously committed persons, socially or environmentally conscious groups, and others concerned with humanity's future.

Bruce O'Hara, Victoria-based consultant and author of *Working Harder Isn't Working*, is Canada's loudest voice in the Shorter Work Time movement, and, for a heady moment in the winter of 1997, British Columbia Premier Glen Clark added his support to the thirty-two-hour work week as something worth considering to reduce unemployment. O'Hara points out that the SWT idea is hardly new.

> Historically, shorter work times have been our primary and most effective tool for keeping unemployment low. Over the period between 1800 and 1950, the standard work week was reduced by an average of three hours every decade. It was understood that labour-saving technology would lead to unemployment and overproduction (and hence a stagnant and depressed economy) if it wasn't offset by a reduction in work times. Starting in the 1950s, economists abandoned this proven approach, embracing instead the hypothesis that growth alone could create full employment.

Of course the growth bubble burst, resulting in today's twin plagues of overwork and underemployment. Go ahead and pick one: fatigue, or poverty? Either way, you suffer, as does your family, and your community. With the social safety net increasingly compromised by debt-ridden governments, millions of people are in need of support from friends and neighbours, yet those who can afford to give it are often too busy or stressed to heed the call. *Noblesse oblige* is a faint memory of more civilized times. These days, most of us escape our duty to community by pleading tired and retreating to our homes.

But avoiding our duty to family is much harder, and this is what's tearing so many of us apart. "The 40-hour work week was designed for men with stay-at-home wives," writes O'Hara:

> When one partner works 40 hours a week outside the home, and the other works a comparable amount of time inside the home, it's a manageable workload. Unfortunately, most of today's full-time workers have a spouse who is also employed full-time, or no spouse at all. At the end of the workday, we come home to the second shift: housework,

childcare, grocery shopping and laundry. It doesn't matter how well we manage that whopping great increase in the family workload: it's always too much, and we pay for it in lives of quiet desperation.

One way to envision a rosier future is to study what a progressive government was able to achieve in the Netherlands. In 1980 that country was in economic turmoil — the result of two decades' steady rise in union wages, widespread unemployment and crippling welfare debt. Today, thanks to ambitious public works programs and a wage-saving consensus between unions and workers, unemployment is stable at 6.5 per cent, the welfare rolls have been cut in half, and the national economy is buoyant. Of all new companies setting up shop in Europe, 45 per cent come to the Netherlands.

> **Some analysts project that within the next decade fewer than 50 per cent of the Canadian workforce will be engaged in full-time, salaried employment.**

Essential to this formula are wage freezes and even reductions, resulting from a large swing to part-time shifts: About one-third of Dutch workers have part-time jobs; and even those working full-time are limited, in many workplaces, to a thirty-three-hour week. Annual vacations average five weeks. Most workers, though poorer than they might have been under the old-style union contracts, are not complaining because for many of them, the alternative is not old-style work but welfare. In the new Netherlands, under a coalition government that combines left, center and right parties, millions of people have settled happily into a routine of working less, living more.

Importing such ideas from Europe will be an uphill battle, given the strong North American resistance to state interference in market forces. Here, we are increasingly led to believe that a strong economy will create its own jobs — that the state should not be in the job-creation or wage-legislation business. Legislating the right to work shorter hours is "nonsense," according to Michael Walker, executive director of Vancouver's conservative think-tank, the Fraser Institute. Flexible work options and banned overtime can only punish employers and in the end, dull the edge of Canadian companies attempting to compete in global markets, says Walker, who believes that ultimately such reforms will undermine the long-term security of employees.

Fortunately, not all business analysts are so intractable. David Brown, senior policy analyst at the Canadian Chamber of Commerce, believes a work-redistribution policy might wash with employers, if it was sweetened by government incentives such as payroll-tax relief. And Frank Reid, a widely quoted University of Toronto economist, envisions a middle-of-the-road solution. Instead of banning overtime, he says, we might consider legislation that supports workers' rights *not* to work. Through an employment-standards law, employees would be empowered to reduce their hours, and employers obliged to accommodate them, just as they already do on issues surrounding parental leave. A moderate approach, in other words, would not so much grant the state power to control workers' lives, as grant workers the right to control their own lives.

Aside from Glen Clark's brief foray into the Shorter Work Time debate, most Canadian politicians have remained cautiously quiet. But there can be no doubt that the debate will gain momentum as disgruntled workers make their votes count. And the ranks of the disgruntled, flanked by the just-plain-confused, are certain to swell in the years ahead as the definition of "work" continues to be rewritten. Some analysts project that within the next decade fewer than 50 per cent of the Canadian workforce will be engaged in full-time, salaried employment. While this might be bad for some people's peace of mind, it will be very good for political consciousness raising. There will be plenty of openings to voice our concerns, and opportunities to lend support to worthwhile initiatives.

In fact, such opportunities already exist — and not just within the ranks of the Shorter Work Time movement. In the spring of 1997, federal health minister David Dingwall announced the government's "intention" to extend medicare to include home-care support for families looking after sick or aging relatives. Not only would this alleviate the pressure on sandwich-generation women, who are often forced to fit home care into their hectic work/family schedules, but it would reduce unemployment in the nursing sector. Win, win. Those of us who understand the enormous difference such changes can make in our lives must make sure these *intentions* become a reality.

HOW TO PUT YOUR WORK IN ITS PLACE

To make a radical change at work, we must take a run at our preconceptions about work. This is a much harder job than most people do in the course of a working day. Workplace culture conspires to keep us on the straight and narrow, urging us to follow our job descriptions to the letter, essentially doing today what we did yesterday, last month, last year. What's called for is a road map to radical territory — a place where our job descriptions fit our life descriptions. To help you get your bearings, here are four essential lessons to help you put work in its place:

- Retirement is no reward.
- Downsizing is not so scary.
- Personal growth is prosperity.
- Ultimately, you're the boss.

Retirement is no reward. A friend of mine, a forty-seven-year-old woman who has been considering leaving her job for longer than I was even *in* mine, recently told me she had solidified an exit plan. She would work for another five years, sock away as much money as possible, then quit. By this time, her two children would be in college and her mortgage would be paid down to the point where her husband, a middle manager, would be able to cover costs. There was nothing terribly creative about this plan, my friend admitted, but it did offer a good shot at early retirement, orchestrated to a theme of financial security. "I know exactly how much I need to live on every year from age fifty-two to sixty-five, when my retirement plans kick in," she told me. "In five years, I'll have that much. I'll never have to work again!"

I flashed her my best "I'm so happy for you" smile, which was hard given the fact my jaw had dropped. She was planning to stay another five years at a company she'd been itching to leave for a decade. That seemed an awfully high price to pay for eventual freedom — for the luxury of "never having to work again." What if she got to that shimmering pot of gold after five more joyless years only to discover it was filled with fool's gold? What if she discovered that the opposite of working is not freedom; it's simply *not* working, and it's *not* for her? What if it took her that long to figure out it was actually her *job* she hated, not her work? That she might have found some perfectly productive way to spend those same five years, working in a different place or in a different way, earning just enough money to keep on living a productive life — for who knows how long? After all, who knows how long life will be? Indeed, the worst *what if* could send anybody's five-year plan into the shredder overnight — and so much for the pay-off.

I'm not suggesting you should do exactly what you want to do every moment of your life because you could drop dead tomorrow. That would hardly be practical. But there is a logical flaw in accepting any and all means to an end when, ultimately, the end is anybody's guess. What's called for is a balanced perspective that brings those means into focus and puts freedom within our grasp, whether it's freedom inside or outside of the workforce. Sticking with work just to get to the end of it is like strapping ourselves to the rack for the wonderful feeling of freedom when the torture is over.

Nor am I suggesting that early retirement is bad for everyone. It obviously does work well for some people, though not as many as those "Freedom 55" financial planners would like us to think. For a great number of working people, including affluent ones, early retirement isn't the answer. Once we've put ourselves out to pasture (or been put there), freedom's glow can tarnish quickly. What in the world do I do once the honeymoon of retirement is over? Within a year, maybe two, I'll have come through the decompression stage, my energy will be restored, my wanderlust sated, my patience for hobbies and socializing worn thin. Suddenly I find myself looking for something to occupy my time. Something like *work*, as a matter of fact — though this time I'm likely to do it on my own terms and enjoy it that much more. If I'm smart and a bit lucky, I'll even be paid for it. So why didn't I figure this out sooner? Because it was hard to think straight while I was stretched on that rack.

The grass of freedom looks greener from the employed side of the fence, so much greener that even the most unreasonable and self-defeating strategies may appear perfectly acceptable so long as they land us on the other side. When we quit this wishful thinking, we notice a growing crowd of retirees looking wistfully back at us from the other side. In their eyes, we're still young(ish), still earning, still growing, still able to contribute to society through hard work done well. What they've learned, and we can learn sooner, is that the kingdom is indeed inside — and so is freedom.

Not surprisingly, demographers have recently spotted the beginnings of an early-retirement backlash, especially among managers and professionals. Perhaps it's too early to call this a full-fledged trend, but Statistics Canada's 1994 General Social Survey showed a steady growth in the numbers of retirees who have turned around and headed back to work within eighteen months of leaving it. Early retirees are twice as likely to do so: roughly one-fifth of women and one-third of men returned to some form of work following early retirement, according to the 1994 survey, and the majority did so for reasons of "personal preference" rather than financial hardship. "Retirement is now much more a change of pace than a fixed point in time where you stop working and never work again," notes Canadian pension expert Monica Townson. With a longer life expectancy, she says, "you're not going to spend one-third of your life doing nothing."

This bodes well for the future, says demographer David Foot, who is happy to see the line between working and not working blurred. In his book *Boom, Bust & Echo*, Foot advocates the establishment of a flexible workforce that values its most knowledgeable and experienced workers. The optimal solution, says Foot, is gradual retirement.

> Those in their late 50s could be working four days a week, after which they would gradually shorten their work week until they are working only one day a week by their early 70s. They could start drawing a partial pension at 55 but would not reach full pension eligibility until 75. In this way, they could remain productive members of the workforce into their 70s, gradually retire with dignity, be present to mentor younger workers, and help reduce the pressure on the Canada Pension Plan.*

Gradual retirement may be a healthy way to look at the latter years of our working life, but that's still a partial solution. How about the first two or three decades? What's called for is a *lifetime* strategy, one that encourages an attitude of constant reinvestment in our careers from the earliest years of work. Let's coin a phrase for this strategy: *serial retirement.* Consider what a positive spin this strategy will give to the notion of leaving work: we're leaving not because we're getting old, or tired, or redundant, but because we're ready to reinvent ourselves.

Demographers have recently spotted the beginnings of an early-retirement backlash, especially among managers and professionals.

The emphasis is much more on returning to work than on leaving it, and when we return we're recharged, perhaps retrained, certainly refocused, ready for new challenges.

You could say serial retirement is a way to embrace the sabbatical spirit, without the seven-year wait. You take a break when you need it, or when your career needs it. Underlying this strategy is the understanding that your career — your life's work — is more than just a

*Reprinted with permission from *Boom, Bust & Echo*, by David K. Foot with Daniel Stoffman; published by Macfarlane, Walter & Ross, Toronto, 1996.

job. Your career is a lifetime investment which (just like money) needs active management to make it grow. Let the equity sit in one place for too long and it's bound to stagnate, eventually to shrink.

Nice theory, but will it work? Unfortunately, there are no guarantees that if I take a break from my current job I'll be able to find a better one. I might wind up with a stack of rejections from employers who couldn't care less whether I'm a "serial" or "permanent" retiree. To them, I'm just out of work, and getting older. This is not a pretty picture, nor is it an uncommon one today. As a 1997 study on Canada's greying labour force concluded, it doesn't matter whether you are forty-seven or sixty-two years old: If you are out of work, you are viewed by most employers as "over the hill." Such job bias flies in the face of evidence to the contrary. Older workers often have much more to offer companies than younger, less experienced ones, says Ivan Hale, executive director of the Toronto-based public interest group One Voice, which commissioned the study. "The country that can harness the talents of its older population will have the competitive edge economically, with the added benefit of enhanced quality of life for its older citizens," Hale reported. His findings suggest Canada is far from becoming one such country: An overwhelming number of employers surveyed reported their belief that older workers have low productivity and should step aside to make way for younger ones. Such bias results in many older workers abandoning their job search, often resorting to self-employment, which, as Hale points out, "is perhaps a euphemism for not working in some instances."

All of which points to the care required in managing our evolving careers. Allowing fear to paralyse the evolution is not the answer. Living in fear of losing your job is often the best way to lose that job — because you stop taking risks and turn into a deadbeat employee. No, we must embrace change, but make our moves wisely, at the right time, with solid preparation and a secure fall-back. In fact, many people find that the preparation stages bring greater rewards than the leave taking, that it may not even be necessary to leave the job. It may be sufficient just to *think about the job differently*. Knowing that you are not likely to stay there until you're sixty-five, come hell or high water, will set you free from treadmill behaviour and allow you to put more energy and passion into your job each day.

Downsizing is not so scary. Fear makes conservatives of the best of us, erecting emotional barriers to change. When an entire society seems to be running scared, those barriers can appear insurmountable. But the reality is that fear usually drives us to do precisely the opposite of what we should do. And the sad thing is that our fears — at least in this case — are largely groundless. They spring more from the uncertainty of the times than from the actual hazards, which are not much different from the hazards of living and working a decade ago, or two, or three. That's not to say uncertainty is easy to live with. For those of us who are insecure, uncertainty is a jagged pill. For those who are blessed with the gift of self-confidence, uncertainty spells opportunity. (Check your own confidence in the future on page 60.)

"Part of the problem is that many of the traditional ideals we were raised on are now suspect," wrote *Utne Reader* executive editor Marilyn Berlin Snell in a preface to that magazine's special section on quitting in September 1996. "We're no longer sure, for instance, whether industriousness is a virtue or a vice; or whether despair is a sin, a medicable illness, or a rational response to an insane world." Significantly, Berlin Snell threw caution to the wind and quit her job at the magazine shortly after shipping that issue to press. (See Ex-File, page 58.)

Social theorist Frank Furedy argues that caution is not the answer, and despair is not a rational response. By allowing our fears to paralyse us, we only promote our own anxiety.

Those who propose to avoid risks and gain safety will invariably find that what they acquire instead are obsessions. Today the fear of taking risks is creating a society that celebrates victimhood rather than heroism. The virtues held up to be followed are passivity rather than activism, safety rather than boldness. And the rather diminished individual that emerges is indulged on the grounds that, in a world awash with conditions and crises and impending catastrophe, he or she is doing a good job just by surviving.

So it's the individual who is being diminished, not just the payroll. *There's* a new definition for downsizing, and a far more disturbing one than we've heard before. In fact, many analysts are now saying that the psychological toll of downsizing is greater than the bottom-line job loss — that what is really going on is large-scale corporate fear-mongering. Jobs have been lost, no question. But more often than not, jobs have been juggled with very little long-term change to the payroll *or* the profits. Recessions always bring lay-offs, and now that the dust is settling on the last one, we can see that the net job loss was not nearly as staggering as we were led to believe — or at least no worse than what we've been through several times before. From 1978 to 1993, according to Statistics Canada, the number of workers permanently laid off each year varied little. In 1982, during the worst of that recession, 1,205,000 Canadians were laid off. In 1989, when the economy was booming, the figure was 1,137,000. In 1991, when recession hit again, it rose slightly to 1,284,000. These are the permanent lay-offs. The temporary ones follow the same pattern of minor variation.

> **Today a job change need not entail a step up—it's okay just to step sideways. Inclusion, not exclusion, is the new ideal . . .**

What the surveys also show, however, is a steep drop in the number of people who leave jobs voluntarily during recessionary times. We're less likely to quit during down times because the perception is that fewer employers are hiring — which is true, but not by much. On average, the hiring rate from 1978 to 1993 was 22 per cent, meaning that about one-fifth of all jobs turned over every year. Hirings were down to 18 per cent in 1991–1993, but have since climbed back over 20 per cent. Now that the economy is well into recovery, the job picture is certainly no worse than it's been in two decades, and salaries are starting to climb after years in the doldrums.

What was the great recession of the early 1990s about? Not reducing numbers, but eliminating expensive "dead wood." Many well-paid, benefit-toting senior employees were replaced by junior staffers and/or contract workers willing to put in longer hours for lower pay and fewer benefits. On paper, that looked like a good deal for employers willing to tap the swelling ranks of non-standard or "contingent" workers to fill the holes left by the retreating dinosaurs. In reality, though, it was a lousy trade. For the short-term rewards of flexibility, they kissed trust, continuity, and staff morale goodbye. Strategic planning took a nosedive. Creativity? Wisdom? Gone with the wind. The prospect of competing in the global economy suddenly looked worse than ever.

Add the questionable logic of downsizing to the questionable morality of the downsizers, and we have a trend whose time is up. People everywhere are outraged, and, in a play for our votes, politicians of all persuasions have lately struck up a chorus of protest against those lean-and-mean business practices. Legislation has been promised to halt layoffs and raise labour standards in many states and provinces across North America. The British Columbia government is looking at ways to legislate basic benefits and insurance packages for contingent employees, which means employers will soon be paying a premium for the privilege of using temp staff for temp jobs, as they should. Many employers will no doubt take this as a cue to rebuild their full-time staffs, and re-establish trust in the bargain.

But one thing they're not likely to rebuild is their management ladder — at least, not if they're smart. Today's corporate leaders are flattening their organizational pyramids. Think of Bill Gates and his plaid-shirted Microsoft managers, all hunkered down in their bare-bones executive cubby holes. You don't climb up in an organization like this; you spiral upward, manoeuvring through a series of lateral leaps that broaden your talents and keep you on a learning curve. No fast track to success here, but plenty of satisfaction on a long and winding road characterized by constant change.

This is a more inviting scenario, especially for managers who've been hamstrung on the old ladder to success. Today a job change need not entail a step up — it's okay just to step sideways. Sometimes, in fact, it's necessary to step down, turn around, and go up a different way. Or forget going up entirely. If social analyst Sally Helgesen is right, the new architecture of business is a web, not a tower, with leaders in the centre and ambitious workers spiralling *in*ward. Inclusion, not exclusion, is the new ideal, and satisfaction the new meaning of success.

So, as we refocus our sights from the joy of climbing to the joy of changing, we can wholeheartedly embrace the change in the world around us. Whether we call it downshifting, rightsizing, delayering, or restructuring, we can start seeing it as an opportunity, not an obstacle — a chance to make some much-needed change of our own, to move on, to grow. Here, in this radical notion of change, is the cure for the fear of joblessness. It's time to put fear behind us and get on with the business of growing.

Personal growth is prosperity. The ability to keep growing is, in the new paradigm, the key to prosperity. Indeed, it *is* prosperity. In an age when financial rewards are unpredictable at best, the rewards of personal growth become paramount. There's a wonderful confluence of the public and the private in this: The more you grow, the greater your rewards — in your life *and* your work. But that's how it ought to be, when the two are happily married.

In your private world, growth may feel like a luxury. In the work world, increasingly, it is a basic survival strategy. Those with outdated skills or a half-baked education are the most vulnerable in these high-tech times. In his book *Boom Bust & Echo*, demographer David Foot notes that in 1994, 145,000 jobs disappeared for Canadians who had no more than a high-school diploma, while 422,000 jobs were created for workers with postsecondary degrees. "Virtually everybody with a postsecondary degree who entered the job market in 1994 got a job, although not always in their area of expertise," writes Foot, who goes on to question whether the word *job* even has a place in the modern lexicon.

Jobs were developed during the 19th century, when factories required units of labour to do the same tasks over and over again. In the information age, workers will apply a wide range of skills to an ever-changing series of tasks, rather than occupying a particular job. While routine tasks are being taken over by machines, non-routine ones still need people to do them. These people will need strong generic skills that can be applied to the many different challenges they will face during their careers.*

What are those generic skills? Literacy is one. Adeptness at team-work is another. Add computer skills (upgraded constantly), top it with the ability to solve problems by thinking analytically, and there you are: Employee of the Month. If you think I'm only talk-ing about "brain" work here, well, I am. Because most work is brain work now — even those jobs we used to call manual labour. Today, manufacturers are looking for skilled people who can work well with their brains as well as their hands, and they're not turning away qualified applicants. In fact, many industrial employers are complaining about the dearth of suitable applicants — of shop foremen who can think analytically, of machinists with strong interpersonal skills. Are these employers' expectations too high? Not in the late 1990s, not if they want to compete in the global market, and win.

Info-tech is not all that's invaded the shop floor. So have women, and for good reason. As automation increases, the need for muscle has been overtaken by the need for the same combination of skills women have always applied to their work, both at home and on the other kind of shop floor — the pink-collar ghetto of the service sector. We women have long suspected ourselves of being the supe-rior sex when it comes to communication, interpersonal, and organi-zational skills. Now, finally, our hunch is being confirmed by the

*Reprinted with permission from *Boom, Bust & Echo*, by David K. Foot with Daniel Stoffman; published by Macfarlane, Walter & Ross, Toronto, 1996.

rewards we're reaping right across the workplace. Thanks to shifts in the economy, and to pressure from the women's movement, barriers are starting to break down between white- and blue- and pink- collar sectors, and slowly but steadily the best women are rising to the top alongside the best men. In Canada for example, two of the big three auto makers now have female presidents: Bobbie Gaunt at Ford and Maureen Kempston Darkes at General Motors.

"Women who have run an organization as complex and constantly changing as a household may be specially well adapted to the confusing multiplicity of the dejobbed world," writes William Bridges in his book *Job Shift*. He points to women like Jane Hirsh and Frances Hesselbein as exemplary. Hirsh went from being staff pharmacist at a hospital to president of the highly successful Copley Pharmaceuticals, a Massachusetts company she started in the 1970s when she needed a job that allowed her to have a crib in her office. While raising six children, she built Copley into a huge enterprise, 51 per cent of which she sold to Hoechst Celanese for $546 million a few years ago. Hesselbein, who never had a paid job until she was over forty, drew from her experiences as homemaker and Scout leader in her home town of Johnstown, Pennsylvania, to become national executive director of The Girl Scouts in 1976, overseeing a professional staff of 500 and a volunteer workforce of 750,000.

Of course these powerhouse women are still the exception to the rule. Statistically, most of women's employment gains in recent years have been in service-related sectors, which puts us on the lower end of the pay scales but compensates us, somewhat, in the sheer volume of job opportunities. "Our" sectors have been growing steadily while the male-dominated manufacturing and construction sectors have shrunk, with the result that women have picked up 69 per cent of the roughly half a million jobs added to the Canadian workforce between 1990 and 1996. Specifically, women grabbed 85 per cent of the new managerial and administrative jobs, 84 per cent of new teaching jobs, and 71 per cent of new medical and health jobs.

So there is reason for optimism, providing we can market those skills that appear to be so perfectly female, and so right for the times. Often, the only missing ingredients are the confidence and connections to sell ourselves effectively. We'll spend more time talking about those ingredients in the chapters ahead. For now, it's enough to know where we *can't* use those qualities: in a job where we're still stuck, trembling, on a ladder.

Ultimately, you're the boss. Now that we understand that the 1990s have been more of a talent juggle than a drain, it's time to get on with the work of developing our own talents. Or it might be more a case of finding suitable outlets for talents and skills that are already well developed but have been underutilized in go-nowhere jobs. That the time is right for this kind of personal development becomes obvious when we examine the areas of business that are growing most dramatically today. The upside of downsizing is the emergence of smaller, smarter companies led by talented men and women who were not so much laid off as set free.

"Guess what happens when a company cuts loose several thousand vigorous and talented knowledge workers? Many start their own companies," writes business consultant Nuala Beck in her book *Excelerate*. This, says Beck, is what happened in the Canadian oil and gas industry a few years ago. When the price of oil collapsed in 1986, several large oil companies responded by quickly downsizing to secure their margins and tide them over until prices returned to "normal." Dead wrong, says Beck. While the big firms waited, their ex-executives were positioning themselves at the helm of junior oil and gas

> **Although many employers are moving away from the old values of loyalty and job security, they depend more than ever on human capital . . .**

companies — small, agile operations capable of quick response to changing indicators. Many leaped boldly into natural gas, which they guessed would be the fuel of choice for the 1990s. Dead right.

And so downsizing has evolved into rightsizing, where the key lesson learned from the recessionary wars is that it's not how big or small you are, it's how smart. A company has to be the right size to get the most from both its leaders and its workers, and the relationship between them is the key to both performance and satisfaction. And not only companies need to be smart, today. We all have to get smart, and start thinking like the boss.

Of course this has always rung true for entrepreneurs, but now it's true for every working person. Each member of the team, while committed to collective goals, ultimately runs her own agenda. While this may appear to contradict the imperative of teamwork, there is in fact no contradiction. I am loyal first and foremost to myself, and am always poised to move on as the task and timing requires. This is not selfishness, nor does it imply disloyalty to my company. What it says is: If I'm going to do a good job here, I need the power and permission to do it right. That is, to do it for the company — but on my terms, and up to my standards.

Empowering workers to do their best work requires empowered management and a new kind of contract between employer and staff. It doesn't matter whether the staff is full-time, part-time, or occasional — the spirit of the contract is the same, and so is the goal: to improve performance by acknowledging, and honouring, the employee's ownership of her work. To do this, the smart organization must take a personal interest in each employee, to determine her areas of expertise and give her greater decision-making authority within those areas. This is how responsibility for performance is shared by manager and employees: through the understanding that shifting control increases empowerment, the net gain being a much higher level of performance all the way through the organization.

What we know about empowered management we have learned, largely, from the knowledge industry, where innovation is a survival tool and where success for the past decade has depended on a high degree of creative teamwork. The success of such approaches is trickling down now to other sectors, as employers increasingly recognize the primacy of knowledge as a tool. As management guru Peter

Drucker points out, 40 per cent of us are now paid not for our labour but for our knowledge, and that percentage is rising fast — the increasingly cheap and plentiful microchip having supplanted the human hand in driving the machines of our economy.

All of this is very good news for women, says Nuala Beck. "Women have landed in the right part of the economy at the right point in history." The ratio of male to female knowledge workers (engineers, scientists, technicians, professionals, and managers) was three to two in 1983. Today it is almost one to one, which means that even as the service sector shrinks in the years ahead — as it is destined to do as a result of increasing automation — women will continue to gain a stronger foothold in the evolving workforce.

The knowledge revolution has fundamentally changed the organizational ideal, says management analyst Charles Handy. Today's model organization is a "membership community," which tends to suit the female work ethic better than the male. "In order to hold people inside the corporation, we can't really talk about their being employees any more," says Handy. And this is the paradox at the heart of the new work world: Although many employers are moving away from the old values of loyalty and job security, they depend more than ever on human capital — on the energy and brains and dedication of their best workers. The smart organizations, the ones that have created a sense of cross-ownership between employee and employer, are the ones that embrace this paradox in order to get to performance.

What does this mean for me? That I can be rented, but not owned. That it's my responsibility to make myself worth renting, by becoming as good at my work as I can, and that in return I can expect to be treated as a valuable member of my work community. This gives me the power I need to set my own rules and limits at work — to call the shots, and even to name my hours. If I know I can fulfil my responsibilities in a thirty-hour week, or a four-day, forty-hour week, or by telecommuting, that's for me to prove and for my employer to acknowledge. More than ever, I have the power to negotiate my own work contract — an essential step towards working less and living more. (See Chapter 6 for practical help on negotiating work options.)

EX-FILE | *The Prosecutor on Pause*

NAME: Linda Wrigley, 44

EX: Senior Crown attorney

CURRENT: Time out

RÉSUMÉ HIGHLIGHTS: Degrees in French, Linguistics, Law; English teacher at junior high, 1978–81; Crown prosecutor, violent crime section, 1985–90; commercial crime section 1990–96.

PERSONAL: Married; one daughter, Saralyn, five.

BACKGROUND: Since I was sixteen years old, I have never *not* had a job, except when I was at law school. When I had the baby, I took an eight-month leave, but I was happy to go back. I just didn't have the personality, I guess, to spend all day long with an eight-month-old baby. I was never one to do the *mom* thing — I couldn't bear to go to showers. I quit my own prenatal class, as a matter of fact — couldn't *stand* it! My feeling, when Saralyn was tiny, was that a nanny would be better at that than I was. It's different now that Saralyn is four: I really feel more need, and desire, to be with her. But that's just half of it; I also needed a change, professionally. I'm a person who needs change — I've studied a lot of different things, I've taught, I've been a lawyer now for ten years, and who knows what's next? I've considered moving into mediation, or arbitration — or I could turn around and do something completely different.

Taking a break like this is a tremendous privilege, but that's not the end of the story. Dugal and I have worked really hard for a long time, and we've been very careful about money. We never allowed ourselves to go and spend a lot of money just because we'd worked hard for it. We paid our mortgage off as soon as we could, and we've never bought expensive things

— clothes, cars, most of our things are pretty basic. Even small things like those little juice boxes that have two sips in them: I buy the big jugs of juice at Costco, and pour it into little plastic containers. You know, it all adds up. So when I see people complain that they're trapped, financially, and then I see them buy a lot of stuff they probably don't need, or run off to Hawaii because they're so burned out from work that they think they've earned a vacation whether they can afford it or not — well, that *is* a trap. Unfortunately, our whole culture feeds that kind of thinking.

I have always put a lot of importance on having my own financial security. I still do. Just knowing all the things that can happen: your husband dies, runs off with his secretary — whatever happens, I have to be financially able to take care of myself. A few years ago, I wouldn't have considered quitting even though my husband was making a good income. Being in his position, Dugal's income could change any time — there's no security there. I had to be secure in my own mind that I had enough of a cushion to carry me through a few years without having to scramble. Now, all of a sudden, both of us aren't working — who would have ever guessed? [Dugal quit his job as vice-president of a real estate development company shortly after Linda's exit from the Crown, claiming he was not influenced by her move and leaving his wife shaking her head in dismay.] But all those years of being careful with our money is paying off now. We'll both be working again soon, no doubt — but we sure are enjoying our freedom in the meantime. Right now, Dugal is down the road playing hopscotch with Saralyn and one of her friends.

WHY I QUIT: I've always made decisions from my head, always been very intellectual in the way I look at things, reasoning everything out carefully. This time it was different. On an intellectual level, everything told me I had a great job — I was senior counsel, had the corner office, I worked part-time, had lots of flexibility — but my gut told me I had to quit. I was feeling dissatisfaction with my accomplishments there. In my own perception I wasn't being very useful. There were a lot of frustrations with the system — the kind of energy I would put into things, just to see it sort of dissipate. An example would be preparing a Supreme Court trial and arriving at court and having it adjourned for a year, when I had just spent two months preparing the case. And I think, okay, I've just spent how many months now? And I'm going to have to do it all again? So, I've just wasted two months of my life because of some little thing that's come up that the defence wants to check into. Or some guy is in custody after embezzling I don't know how many hundreds of thousands of dollars, and they just keep adjourning it, and letting him out so he can keep doing the same thing again and again. It's just not dealt with fast enough. That's a huge frustration.

In violent crime, it's more of an emotional drain — a lot of negative energy coming at you. You're dealing with a sex assault one day and a stabbing the next, a rapist the next, and you're fighting with some judge who's being a jerk. Eventually you simply burn out — it happens to everyone. I found myself taking the easy route instead of fighting as I used to. In the last few years, I'd negotiate a guilty plea at any cost. Well, not any cost — but you compromise at the expense of some justice, and that tears at your conscience.

But I can't say I left because I had a bad job — that's not it. It was my own growing and changing that made it hard to stay. I had an ideal work situation, as a lot of women have with the Crown — much more so than for lawyers in private practice. I had maximum flexibility. Since Saralyn was born, I worked three days a week and had total control of how I used that time, so that I could make sure the whole week was covered. Flexibility doesn't mean you should put your needs ahead of your job. The job still comes first, which is why I had a full-time nanny. If I had a two-week trial, I was there for two weeks.

Of course, full-time childcare for a part-time job is an extremely inefficient way to earn a living. And then there's the tax bite! I once worked it out that I was netting $800 a month, which makes you think twice about whether it's worth your time. Up until the end, I'd have to say yes, it was worth it. It was a great job — but I had reached maximum satisfaction there.

THE TURNING POINT: I was probably ready to quit for over a year, but I was wrestling with myself over what that would mean to my self-esteem. Working had always been the clear choice for me. I wasn't interested in falling into that female role — playing second fiddle to men all the time, and having the economic disadvantage, and not having the impact, the power, the importance that an active role in the workforce gives you. I don't think I've really changed my position on this. I wouldn't have been able to quit had I not had a huge measure of impact at my work. Actually it was Dugal who said to me, "We know you can do it. We know you're a big downtown lawyer, we know you can win a major Supreme Court case — you don't have to *keep* doing it." It was a revelation to me, that if I stopped doing it I wouldn't lose a huge measure of my identity. I still seem to use my work to identify myself — maybe I'll always be that way — but now when someone asks me what I do, I say, well, this is what I've done, and I've done it for so many years, and I'm taking some time off now. This might not work for me five years from now, but by then I'll probably be doing something else, anyway.

TAKE-OUT WISDOM: In the last few months, when I was preparing to leave, I made a scrapbook of all my cases and the newspaper articles and commendation letters and my own notes and thoughts — it was a catharsis, a way for me to feel I was wrapping up that part of my life. It sounds kind of sad, but it was a very happy experience.

EX-FILE | *The Escape Artist*

NAME: Marilyn Berlin Snell, 38

EX: Executive Editor

CURRENT: Freelance writer; editor

RÉSUMÉ HIGHLIGHTS: B.A., M.A. International Journalism; Senior Editor, *New Perspectives Quarterly* (social/political journal based in Los Angeles), 1987–92; Executive Editor, *Utne Reader* (300,000-subscriber magazine based in Minneapolis), 1994–96.

PERSONAL: Single

BACKGROUND: I did not quit my job to spend more time with my kids (have none), or my partner (I'm as single as it gets outside the nunnery). Nor was I offered a better editorial position elsewhere. I quit because I could — I've got savings and a supportive network of family and friends — and because I despaired of becoming what I knew lay at the end of the road I was travelling: a superficial, passionless, and formulaic journalist whose pay cheques are regular but whose heart and brain are still as death.

HOW I QUIT: The decision was easy. After two years at a magazine that presented itself to the reading public one way and comported itself internally quite another, and after it hired as editor-in-chief someone from *People* magazine who seemed more concerned with captions than with editorial content, I decided that my spiritual and mental health depended upon my resignation. As my final act I conceptualized and edited an issue titled "Just Quit! The Fine Art of Breaking Free." It was a premeditated act of performance art, the only way I could see of making something good and perhaps even useful out of what had become intolerable for me. I understand that this issue has sold like hot cakes, which leads me to conclude that I did indeed extricate myself with some semblance of grace (in business, there's nothing more graceful than profit). And then I got in my car and headed west, as Americans have always done when they're searching for their promised land.

THE PROMISE: For me, the promise lay in writing stories about people who are complex and representative of a changing American landscape, people full of search and struggle and glimmers of charity, as well as a growing humility and even despair. This is the real America, one that our mainstream mags prefer to ignore. I don't know if I can make any money telling these stories but for now, I'd have to say that I'm more inspired about my line of work, more creatively engaged and excited to begin each day, than I've ever been. It hasn't hurt that I've been offered several freelance editing jobs that will keep the money coming in while I work on what I believe to be my *calling*.

TAKE-OUT WISDOM: I'm proud of what I'm doing, I'm intellectually challenged, and I'm scared as hell and not a little confused about how to proceed. But like the great humanist photographer Henri Cartier-Bresson, who once said that he gets up each day and goes out to take pictures in order to figure out what he thinks, I feel that I live most fully in those moments when I am just trying to figure out what I think about the world around me, when I'm acting out of curiosity, compassion, and a healthy skepticism rather than complacency, formula, or a stupid mandate from my superiors. This may mean no more than that I'm unemployable. I'm willing to take that risk.

CHECK |
Your Career Transition

1. WHAT DOES YOUR FUTURE LOOK LIKE?

Here is an exercise to help clarify your approach to major life change and facilitate decision making. How you view the "shape" of the future deeply influences your ability to make choices that can change the course of your life. Four metaphors are offered, each describing one way of envisioning the future. Read all four, then decide which one most closely matches your view.

Roller Coaster

The future is a great roller coaster on a moonless night. It twists ahead of us in the dark, although we can only see each part as we come to it. We can make estimates about where we are headed, and sometimes see around a bend to another section of track, but it doesn't do us any real good because the future is fixed and determined. We are locked in our seats and nothing we may know or do will change the course that is laid out for us.

Mighty River

The future is a mighty river. The great force of history flows inexorably along, carrying us with it. Most of our attempts to change its course are mere pebbles thrown into the river; they cause a momentary splash and a few ripples, but they make no difference. The river's course can be changed, but only by natural disasters like earthquakes or landslides, or by massive concerted human efforts on a similar scale. On the other hand, we are free as individuals to adapt to the course of history, either well or poorly. Looking ahead, we can avoid sandbars and whirlpools and pick the best path through any rapids.

Great Ocean

The future is a great ocean. There are many possible destinations, and many different routes to each destination. Good navigators take advantage of the main currents of change, adapt their courses to the capricious winds of chance, keep a sharp lookout posted, and move carefully in fog or uncharted waters. If they do these things, they will get safely to the destination (barring a typhoon or other natural disaster that they can neither predict nor avoid).

Colossal Dice Game

The future is entirely random, a colossal dice game. Every second, millions of things happen that could have happened another way and produced a different future. A bullet is deflected by the branch of a tree and kills one person instead of another. A scientist checks a spoiled culture and throws it away, or looks more closely at it and discovers penicillin. A spy at Watergate removes a piece of tape from a door and gets away safely, or he forgets to remove the tape and changes American political history. Since everything is chance, all we can do is play the game, pray to the god of fortune and enjoy what good luck comes our way.

ANALYSIS: There is no "right way" to view the future. Your life experiences to date — and some would say your formative childhood years count most — usually dictate the shape of your perceptions and beliefs. These, in turn, profoundly affect the confidence you bring to the challenge of shaping your life. You may wish the future were an ocean that you could skilfully navigate, but if deep down you believe it's a dice game, then you will need more than navigation skills to get on with change. You will need to find ways to boost your confidence and overcome obstacles such as fear, lethargy, and denial. This doesn't mean you can't be a navigator — just that it may be harder for you. Knowing this from the outset is an advantage. You can set your expectations and your timeline accordingly. A simplified "Resistance Index" is given below (1 indicates you have little innate resistance to change, 4 indicates a good deal of resistance). As with most of the exercises in this book, how far you go with this analysis is entirely up to you. If you are troubled by your own response to this or any other exercise, take it as a cue for further exploration.

Resistance Index

IF YOUR FUTURE IS A	YOUR RESISTANCE TO CHANGE IS
Great Ocean	1
Mighty River	2
Colossal Dice Game	3
Roller Coaster	4

MORE METAPHORS, FOR KEENERS: Think of an accomplishment, hobby, or interest in your life — something that is gratifying and significant to you. It can be playing a musical instrument or taking part in a sport, a cultural group, or a hobby like gardening or collecting antiques. It can also be a workplace activity, such as a leadership role that brings you satisfaction. Visualize the elements that combine to make that experience valuable to you — the practice, the rules, the social elements, the traditions, and the rewards. Now use that experience to create a metaphor for career change.

For example, someone who golfs might say:

■ *Making a career change is like playing golf because you must keep your eyes on the ball and keep moving ahead towards your goals.*

If you are an aerobics buff, you might say:

> ■ *Making a career change is like aerobics because you must stay in shape and always be aware of how your moves are affecting the people around you.*

ANALYSIS: This kind of exercise is favoured by vocational counsellors because people tend to successfully internalize, learn, and remember something that can be linked to their daily experiences. The purpose of the exercise is to show how career planning and decision making are much like many of the other activities in our lives. To enrich your work life, why not borrow skills, habits, and approaches that prove most successful in other areas of your life?

Metaphor exercises are adapted from ICDM *Training Materials developed by the Washington State Occupational Information Coordinating Committee.*

2. ARE YOU READY FOR SUCCESS?

Success is a trade off. If you're in the midst of career transition, you've probably already learned this. Success at work can quite easily be gained at the expense of success at home, and vice versa. Much harder to achieve is a balanced kind of success that satisfies you as a whole person — at work and at home. Pipe dream? Not according to the new generation of career counsellors who believe we can, truly, have it all if we embrace the trade off as a good thing — as the key to becoming our own bosses. The balance that comes from taking charge of your life — setting terms that fit your needs and desires — nets greater flexibility, more openness to learning, faster response to change, and, ultimately, a more productive life *and* career.

Most of us are experiencing this sea change by necessity, not choice. Many of the rewards we thought we were working for have vapourized in a work world overshadowed by fear and stress. If we are to find a healthier way to work, we must redefine "success" by creating a new set of rewards for ourselves. Dr. Barbara Moses, a human resources consultant with clients across North America, offers valuable advice in her latest book, *Career Intelligence: Mastering the New Work and Personal Realities* (Stoddart, 1997). She urges clients and readers to measure success not in terms of the traditional rewards, but of the intrinsic qualities of a job: "Is it skill-building? Fun? Challenging? Does it provide opportunities to balance work and personal life? Essentially, people are saying, 'I may no longer be able to aspire to the traditional trappings of success. But that gives me the freedom to make life choices that reflect my needs and values.'"

Moses sets out the following twelve rules of success for the new work world. Though written chiefly for a business clientele, the principles apply to virtually all career endeavours.

- **Be a career activist** Market yourself. Ask yourself if your skills are up to industry standards. Search for opportunities to enhance your marketability and ensure you have a full portfolio of skills. Always make the most of your current work situation, even while planning for the next.
- **Think globally** Cultural and linguistic versatility count. Today's work world is borderless and the whole globe is a potential market. Read international books and magazines, join broadly based associations, and exchange information through the Internet.
- **Hone communication skills** Decentralization of businesses and information overload among managers means you have to do your homework before making a presentation; be able to cut to the quick.
- **Keep on learning** Lifelong learning is not a catchphrase but a necessity. In many companies, upgrading of skills is no longer a shared responsibility. It's yours.

- **Understand business trends** Specialize at your own risk. Keep your knowledge base broad by constantly reading, following trends in economics, demographics, and culture.

- **Prepare for areas of competence, not for jobs** Labour-market projections are notoriously unreliable. Count on your job competency, not on your job title, to keep you competitive.

- **Read the experts with caution** Having an informed market sense will help you cull the real opportunities from today's "hot" sheet. Best bets: continuing education, "edutainment," recreation, and personal services.

- **Build financial independence** Think in terms of having multiple income streams, not a salary. Align your income needs with your personal needs and values. Be ruthless in evaluating how well or badly these are lined up now.

- **Think lattice, not ladders** Today you have to move sideways before you move up. In a lattice, everything is connected.

- **Decide: Are you a specialist or a generalist?** In fact, you need to be both. Strong specialist skills will get you in the door, but generalists have the flexibility to make internal moves. Seek counselling if you need help determining your strengths and dealing with weaknesses.

- **Manage your time** This includes evaluating every time commitment in your life, not just at work. Vigilance is required in saying no, setting priorities, knowing limitations.

- **Be kind to yourself** Don't constantly struggle to attain 100 per cent in every department of life. Remind yourself of successes, nurture a community of people who appreciate you.

THREE

Women's Liberation: The Sequel

THAT WAS THEN	THIS IS NOW
Political	Radical
Labelled	Liberated
Playing a role	Being yourself
Correct choice	Free choice
Us and them	All of us
Feminist politics	Feminist ideals
Self-interest	Common good
Male hegemony	Female advantage
Competition	Connection
Working for	Working with
Hitting your stride	Finding your voice

We've been talking about radical change — how it's the right response in radical times — and we haven't even gotten to the explosive issues of sexual politics. Ready to launch a few missiles? As Bette Davis said in *All About Eve*, "Fasten your seat belts, kids, it's going to be a bumpy night."

For a warm-up, here's something I plucked from cyberspace, right around the time when the so-called family values debate had reached the hard-crack point in the months preceding the 1996 US presidential elections. I kept thinking, during that period, how very odd it is to debate family values — for the Republicans to act as though they owned them, and the Democrats to appear so defensive. I mean, has anyone come out *against* family values? Is Bill Clinton any less a family man for being a Democrat? Is Hillary Clinton any less a mom for being a feminist and day care advocate? And, more to the point, am I a "traditional" woman just because I want to spend more time with my family and less at work? Some women may think this of me, but frankly the traditional label gives me the shivers. To my mind, quitting work was a radical thing to do. Staying there would have been more traditional. But we'll dive into that debate soon enough. First, this e-mail post from a feminist chatline.

As you all know, we have a heck of a time keeping track of the feminist agenda. I know I keep losing it. Evidently I didn't read it very well because Pat Robertson was quoted as saying it is in the agenda that we leave our husbands, kill our children, and become lesbians. My husband will be a little bummed about the lesbian part, but it does make sense about why I never have seen any children around the house. I don't ever remember reading that part, but why would Pat Robertson lie? Anyway, here's our new agenda.

Feminist Agenda

0800–0815	Introduction, Opening Remarks
0815–0915	Plot to Overthrow World Leadership
0915–0930	BREAK — Coffee and Donuts
0930–1030	Undermine World Religions
1030–1200	General Attacks on the Institution of the American Family
1200–1300	Catered Lunch and Fashion Show
1300–1330	Plot to Remove All Men from the World
1330–1400	BREAK — Cake and Champagne

1400–1500	Leave Husbands (If Applicable)
1500–1530	Kill Children
1530–1700	Become Lesbian
1730+	Evening Mixer; Open Bar

Okay, we've had our laugh at the right wing's expense. But before we get too smug, let's look at "family values" and the "feminist agenda" and why more than a few politicians — men and women — have made it their business to pit one against the other, as though to be feminist is to be anti-family. Have feminists brought this disdain upon themselves? Simple answer: yes. Our mistake was to adopt labels (*them* versus *us*) and become slaves to those labels. Although at times I've called myself a feminist, for fear of being labelled a reactionary, I'd sooner torch both labels. These days, moving beyond feminism feels a lot like liberation.

Where did feminism go wrong? Despite crucial gains made through decades of good work, from the early suffrage campaigns to the battles for rights over reproductive control, sexual orientation and workplace equity, the health of the movement has ultimately been undermined by the simple fact of being a "political movement" — and one that purports to speak for half of humanity. To fight for the rights of all women may have seemed a noble goal once upon a time, but of course it turned out to be impractical on a grand scale. The movement, inevitably, turned its energies to fighting for the kinds of things that *can* be fought for within a political framework. The focus became the rights of marginalized women — women of colour, women who have been battered and abused, women who are persecuted for loving other women, women who lack power and opportunity in a workplace still dominated by men.

In fine-tuning itself politically, modern feminism became exclusionist. Sexual revolutionaries such as Betty Friedan and Germaine Greer did not see men as the enemy, but as co-beneficiaries in our liberation battle. It is only in recent years that the battle has been turned into liberation *from* men — into a war against not only male hegemony but also males themselves. By the 1980s, according to feminist critic and author Myrna Kostash, "it had become important for all feminists to affirm lesbian sexuality and visibility. But there was an over-correction of heterocentrism, and the issue of sexual violence overtook that of heterosexual pleasure." As politicized women became more and more focused on our own social, moral, and sexual affirmation, we placed less value on husbands, and consequently in "traditional" family.

Here was the perfect set-up for backlash, for mud-slinging, and for what Kostash calls "the new generation of post-feminist feminists who grieve that it has become difficult to justify theoretically that they are feminists who sleep with men." In us-and-them feminism, women who sleep with the enemy have naturally *become* the enemy — which doesn't bother most women I know because, well, who has the time to grieve? The "movement" has simply become irrelevant to most women, and not only those who've chosen traditional wife/ mother roles. It has also become irrelevant, and even counter-productive, to those who've spent these last decades in dogged pursuit of the old feminist goal of workplace equity. Executive women who may have started out as feminists have found, overwhelmingly, that sexual politics are no more productive in the boardroom than in the bedroom. Ambitious women have had to embrace men, and emulate them, in order to win at their game, because business is still very much a man's sport.

> Ambitious women have had to embrace men, and emulate them, in order to win at their game, because business is still very much a man's sport.

And it's a blood sport, make no mistake. Many of us so-called successful women discovered we were not chasing equality — at least, not equality *for women*. We were chasing equality for ourselves, in a workforce fuelled by greed. Or, more accurately, we were chasing status and power. Self-interest had replaced any sense of the common good. We looked back at the battles we'd fought for sexual equality, pay equity, and social justice as something we did when we were young, before we got busy claiming our place on the ladder. Though some women continue to uphold those ideals, and even to smuggle them bravely into their workplace, few of us do so under the banner of feminism. To do so only confuses and alienates our male colleagues, any number of whom probably believe Pat Robertson's version of the "agenda." So we've tossed the old label and gotten down to the business of earning a living, accepting that when you become the establishment, it's not smart to go around knocking it.

Having accepted the establishment rules, we've done our best to play by them. Good sportsmanship often requires us to smile through grinding teeth, as we do when we accept the rule about power and sex: Power is sexy, when a man holds it. When a woman holds it — well, that's a whole different story. "It is de-eroticizing for men when women are powerful," wrote Judy Rebick in *Canadian Forum*. By complaining about this, as opposed to celebrating it, the former president of the National Action Committee on the Status of Women sets herself apart from the new crop of "gender feminists." Those stridently liberated younger women wouldn't complain about not being seen as sexually desirable by men. The new feminists seem to be happier in the company of women, which is one good reason you don't find many of them in corporate boardrooms. Stridency obviously won't work for those of us who prefer to play the establishment game, where winning against men means accepting the erotic balance of power.

On the corporate playing field, we gain power by wielding grace, charm, and flattery as weapons to attract and empower men, to make them feel good about themselves and, in turn, about us. It's a flirting game, basically, and to do it well we must dig into the old bag of feminine tricks that our more radical sisters burned along with their bras. "I blatantly used my feminine wiles," Tina Knight recently told *The Globe and Mail*. Knight is owner of the British computer manufacturing firm Nighthawk Electronics (annual sales, $5 million). "To get ahead," she says, "you use every opportunity you can in business."

For women who don't know what those opportunities might be, there is no shortage of self-help material on the bookshelves. Harriet Rubin, the New York publisher in charge of the Doubleday Currency business books, has just penned her own, *The Princessa: Machiavelli for Women*. In it she promotes a philosophy of sheer chutzpah, which boils down to: If you want it, get it! And if it works, use it! Rubin's own arsenal includes tears, big jewellery, bright colours, and breasts. Likewise, Karen Salmansohn advocates wielding "cleavage power" on the corporate playing field, and spells out several strategies in her book *How to Succeed in Business Without a Penis: Secrets and Strategies for the Working Woman*.

This is not just a case of authors trying to create a new niche. That businesswomen need to play such games in order to succeed was confirmed in a large-scale survey conducted in 1996 by Catalyst, a non-profit New York–based advocacy and support organization for working women. Close to five hundred women from Fortune 1000 firms responded, many of them complaining about the emotional toll taken by success. To make it, a majority of these women reported they had to mask their differences and strive to be "just like the guys," which meant embracing cocktail culture, learning to follow spectator sports, or taking up golf. And even so, performance expectations remained out of whack for them: 99 per cent of respondents said they had to outperform men in order to reach the same goals.

This macho brand of corporate success is clearly not for everyone, not even for a lot of men. But it's women who are most seriously handicapped in the race to the top of the ladder, and this isn't just because we don't like flirting. (Some of us still do.) It's more a case of being too nice. This is what *Globe and Mail* business editor Margaret Wente calls the X-factor. It's the reason why, despite women's tremendous progress as managers, professionals, and entrepreneurs, there is still a glass ceiling. "Only it's made of cement," wrote Wente in a provocative op-ed column in the fall of 1996. In searching for the X-factor, Wente reviewed and rejected all the usual suspects: exclusionary male culture (we are spectator sports-challenged), the business pipeline (we haven't been in it long enough yet), and children (they take up too much of our time). While these factors do contribute to the ceiling, none of them supply the cement. The big one, the X-factor, is our basic lack of aggression. It's a jungle out there, says Wente, and the largest gorillas win.

> The fact that people behave like primates is not to say that capitalism is such a terrible system. These ferocious, teeth-baring alpha males do, after all, create millions of jobs and billions in shareholder value for nice people such as you and me. But do not expect women to take them on any time soon. Women are not nasty enough.

Sounds simplistic, but Wente's analysis comes as close as anything I've read to explaining why our progress up the ladder has been so slow, despite the dramatic equalization over past decades in the number of male and female graduates entering the workforce. In their 1996 book, *The Futures of Women*, Pamela McCorduck and Nancy Ramsey document this phenomenon, dashing the optimistic feminist view that we're hurtling towards sexual equality. In fact, if the rate of change in the last twenty years holds steady, McCorduck and Ramsey say, men and women will not be equally represented among senior corporate managers of American corporations until the year 2270.

Of course some women have already made it to the top of the ladder, and not because they're nasty people or have too many male hormones. In most cases, it's because they're so brilliant at their job that they don't have to pull any fancy tricks on the way up. But for every one of them, there are hundreds who tire and turn back, or throw themselves off the ladder, disgusted at how narrow their lives are and how deadening the day-after-day power plays of achieving and maintaining position. Is this all there is? they begin to ask. The question is always the prelude to a leap.

And who is there to catch these women when they land? Their male colleagues? Not on your life. It's women who do the reaching out, the catching, the consoling. Women are there for other women, if not as mentors on the way up, then certainly as helpmates on the way down. That's the kind of primates we are. And that is precisely the seed of our much-needed redefinition of feminism. If success, in a man's world, is defined by status, power, and self-interest, then success in a liberated (X-factored) world is defined by reaching out — a *being there* for others: for women, for men, for our families, and our communities.

This is not a question of women going back to being the "supporter" to a husband's or boss's "provider." That's just a backlash. What's required is a rethinking of all the rules, and roles, so that supporters and providers are equally respected and rewarded by our society. This will require an equal mix of self-interest and devotion to the common good, and for us to achieve such a mix, we must all, men and women, contribute to a new bottom line — one that requires us to be more caring and less greedy. Our own health depends upon this, as does the health of our families and, indeed, the continued existence of *civil* society. American political scientist Benjamin Barber, in his book *Jihad Vs. McWorld*, defines civil society as the middle ground between our public and private worlds: "It is not where we vote and it is not where we buy and sell; it is where we talk with neighbors about a crossing guard, plan a benefit for our community school, discuss how our church or synagogue can shelter the homeless."

How do we get to that civil space and become, in turn, good citizens? This is where radical thinking comes alive. Barber's book is radical because he takes all the cards that have been neatly stacked in piles labelled right, left, profit, loss — and tosses them up in the air. He then restacks them according to common-sense values that defy labels, human values that simply work because they foster caring solutions to the everyday problems of life in our communities. For women faced with the wearying contradictions of gender and workplace politics, the radical solution is to toss our cards up in the air with all our might. This ought to take the form of a celebration, because the way we've had them stacked for the last few decades has not proved to be much fun for most of us. We've allowed other people to do the stacking — whether these were men, in the name of profit, or women, in the name of feminism. It's definitely time for each one of us to do some tossing of our own, and to enjoy the few moments of chaos that signal the start of real liberation — of life without labels.

The long-term result of such liberation will be an equalization, both at home and in the workplace, that springs from recognition of the natural strengths and deepest desires of both men and women. In a workforce fuelled by both profit and passion, that caters equally to those who climb and those who care, women will begin taking their rightful place, and in the right numbers. The work world will become a fairer place, and society more civil, when the lion truly sleeps with the lamb — in the boardroom. If we all start working on this today, we're bound to hit "equality" well before the year 2270.

DOING OUR BEST WORK

It takes courage to let go of labels that define and confine us, but that's what we have to do to be good citizens in the company of women and men. Where feminism is concerned, the label has all too often made some women's choices more "correct" than others. Why should not every woman have the right to make informed and dignified choices for herself? This, more than anything, was the ideal upheld by early feminism, and the one from which we've strayed the farthest. We need to go back to such an ideal, and we need to do it for the common good.

> **For many women, the focus of caring has simply shifted to the workplace, because that's where we spend so much of our waking time.**

By throwing our cards up in the air, and by throwing out us-and-them politics in the process, we can liberate ourselves from labels that define correctness according to someone else's agenda. And we can get down to the business of doing our best work. It helps when we find some like-minded women to do this with, because no matter how hard women can be on one another, we still seem to do our best work in groups. Whether by nature or nurture, we're inclined to support, console, and simply be there for one another in ways that come much harder for men.

The natural female urge to work together explains why, for all those women who have fallen away from organized feminism in the last two decades, countless more have fallen together into advocacy and support groups, professional networks, educational councils, social salons, healing circles — all kinds of arrangements that recognize you can't work on the common good all by yourself. There is strength in numbers, and we need that strength in order to have an impact on the "civil space" Benjamin Barber talks about.

That civil space is where people like Lynn Smith live. The dean of law at the University of British Columbia, Smith devotes much time and great skill to smuggling feminist principles into a bastion of male power, and in so doing, has an enormous impact on the lives of those around her. She has opened her faculty to part-time students so those with children can attend, she has been a tireless promoter of research into equality rights, and she has established a chair in Women and the Law at her university. Nationally, Smith is a founding director of the Women's Legal Education and Action Fund (LEAF), a non-profit organization of mostly female lawyers who take on precedent-setting cases on behalf of women under the Charter of Rights and Freedoms. Smith has volunteered her own legal time and resources in dozens of LEAF's landmark cases.

Being an effective civil-space worker is easier if you have a law school behind you — but sometimes just a dining room full of friends is all you need. A group of women in Carleton Place, Ontario, mobilized around their friend Heather Imming a few years ago when her abusive husband threatened to return and "finish the job" on his release from prison. Over coffee and cookies one afternoon, ten of Heather's friends launched the Committee to Protect Heather Imming from Further Violence. They helped Heather install a security system, set up a round-the-clock surveillance of her home, lobbied the courts to keep her husband in jail for his full term, and organized a public safety campaign on behalf of Heather and other victims of abuse.

There are big, public causes like these ones — and there are small, private causes which can be every bit as noble. A friend of mine takes her elderly neighbour grocery shopping once a week. Another runs the bingo program at a seniors' home. Another hosts a new immigrant family for sabbath and holiday dinners. A couple of moms in my neighbourhood stepped in when funding for a crossing guard dried up, and now do this job daily, for free. Nothing revolutionary in these labours of love: our society has always expected women to step in where needed, and women have always obliged. When I was growing up, I often watched my mom dash out the door in her volunteer's smock, heading for a nearby hospital where she and a couple of her "girlfriends" would spend hours visiting sick people, listening to their stories, trying to make them a little more comfortable. Our dads may have done the odd bit of service-club fund-raising, but they never put on a smock. They were too busy at the office.

These days, most women are also too busy at the office. They barely get enough time off to take care of their families, never mind visit a hospital or take a crossing-guard shift. But given the pressures of modern life, it is remarkable what many women do manage to accomplish in the way of good works — *at work*. Dr. Gail Robinson is a fine example. The University of Toronto professor (of psychiatry as well as obstetrics and gynecology) helped found Toronto's Rape Crisis Centre in 1973 and went on to co-found the women's mental health program at U of T — the most comprehensive program of its kind in North America. In a recent interview with writer Val Ross, Robinson articulated her strategy: "We had to make it clear to the administration that this would be a legitimate and scientific field of study, that we could get grants and we could publish," she says. "We felt we could never have presented our case if we'd made it a political thing. The idea was not to challenge the system but to work with the system."

For many women, the focus of caring has simply shifted to the workplace, because that's where we spend so much of our waking time.

With caring in the mix, it doesn't really matter whether we're wearing smocks or suits. And it doesn't matter if we have a place in the board-room or the mail room — there's good work to be done at every level. But the higher you go up the ladder, the more dramatic the results — probably because executive women know how to wield power tools.

A perfect example of pinstriped caring is the women's network at the Canadian Imperial Bank of Commerce, a group profiled by business consultant Tema Frank in her book *Canada's Best Employers for Women*. In the early 1990s, at the bank's Toronto headquarters, a small group of executive women rallied around a colleague who was about to go on maternity leave. They felt she needed and deserved income support, and decided to lobby senior management through an in-house e-mail campaign. It took only a few months for their superiors to recognize that it would be more productive to chan-nel all this female energy than to try to squelch it. The bank launched a program to top up federal unemployment insur-ance benefits for women on maternity

> **The female model is more a web than a ladder, where connection replaces competition, inclusion replaces alien-ation . . .**

leave. A few months after that, the bank's chairman established a Com-mittee on Women's Issues, the benefits of which have trickled down to staff at all levels, including men. Many of the so-called women's issues, after all, concerned employment opportunities and family pri-orities — by no means the exclusive domain of women.

As a result of that lobby group, and the chairman's committee it spawned, CIBC has evolved into one of the most progressive employ-ers in the banking industry. The old promotions pipeline that favoured men, and only certain men at that, has been replaced with an egali-tarian "staffing network" which is proving to be a boon to all moti-vated employees. A variety of flexible work options have been introduced as part of a "Work and Lifestyle" program, and more than a few men are taking advantage of them, alongside their female colleagues. These options include flex hours, telecommuting, job-sharing, and part-time work — even at the managerial level. While the cement ceiling is still in evidence at CIBC, it has definitely been raised a foot or two. Two decades ago, the bank did not even allow female university grads into management training; today, 14 per cent of its senior management are women — one of the highest rates in the banking sector. The number of women in CIBC's middle management has risen from 35 per cent in 1987 to more than 50 per cent today. "A boys' club still exists," said one female manager, "but it is no longer a power club; it is more like a circling of the wagons."

Tema Frank, whose *Best Employers* is a must-read for Canadian women interested in corporate careers, notes that the CIBC women remain guardedly optimistic about their future. She was witness to debates about "whether the CIBC is a women-friendly organization that still has a few bad parts, or not yet a women-friendly organization, with several good parts. Either way," reports Frank, "all agreed that the bank has come a long way and that it is dealing seriously with the parts that need improvement."

This is how a lot of women do their best work today, smuggling their value systems and priorities in through the back door, and quietly celebrating results that are good for everybody. Of course, when they own their own companies, they don't have to smuggle — which goes a long way to explaining the great rise in female-owned businesses over recent years. In her latest book, *The Female Advantage*, Sally Helgesen observes the ways in which women's businesses distinguish themselves from those owned by men. While the male model upholds the lone-wolf ideal of the businessman as hero, female leadership is dedicated to the creation of a community of like-minded workers who share in the fruits of their collective labour. The female model is more a web than a ladder, Helgesen says, where connection replaces competition, inclusion replaces alienation, and the meeting of human needs is always paramount to *efficiency*. Lean and mean is not in the female vocabulary.

"Given the changing nature both of work and of people who work, there emerges a need for leaders who can stimulate employees to work with zest and spirit," writes Helgesen. "Such leaders must create an ambience that reflects human values, and devise organizational structures that encourage and nurture human growth." Dorothy Brunson, the Philadelphia broadcast executive and founder of Associated Black Charities, is a good example, says Helgesen, and even the modest decor of Brunson's flagship TV station, WEBB, underlines the difference between classic male and progressive female leadership: "I want the style of my office to show that I'm not removed," Brunson told Helgesen. "I want my people to feel as if they're part of what's going on. Having lots of fancy things isolates you by proclaiming your status."

While male-led businesses struggle to change with the times, importing therapists, philosophers, and even poets to help them breathe life into their tired hierarchies, female-led businesses are emerging as simply, inherently, right for the times. A 1996 Dun & Bradstreet survey found that nearly one-third of Canadian companies are now run by women — a 20 per cent increase since 1992 — and that these firms are creating jobs at a rate of more than four times the national average. Researchers have found the same trend at work in the United States, where women now own eight million companies — one-third of all businesses in the country. These female-owned companies have significantly better staying power than male-owned firms, and their employment rolls are growing twice as fast as the average. Though there are no statistics, yet, to show that these female entrepreneurs are hiring more women than men to flesh out their growing payrolls, I would hazard a bet that this is true, and that it explains the significant advantage women have over men when it comes to nabbing newly created jobs.

Who are these entrepreneurial women? A few are executive refugees from the boardroom wars. The majority, though, come from middle- and low-salary jobs where opportunities are sorely limited and rewards measured on somebody else's scales. Many emerge from the ranks of the outplaced and destructured, so they start extremely lean. Michelle Paquette, for example, launched Womanpower Renovation out of the basement of her Winnipeg home when she was unemployed. Having offered to help friends with odd jobs in their homes, she understood that many women prefer to do repairs and renovations themselves but don't know how to get started. So she set herself up as a do-it-yourself consultant, teaching her clients the skills they need by doing the work *with* them rather than for them.

Help is on the way for women with big ideas but modest means, and, predictably, it is on the way from other women. In 1996, a partnership of businesswomen launched the Women and Economic Development Consortium, a national philanthropic organization dedicated to helping low-income women start their own businesses. They already have millions in the kitty, and more to come from corporate backers including Levi Strauss & Co., the Bank of Montreal, and the Canadian Alternative Investment Co-operative. In its first year, the consortium hopes to assist as many as six hundred entrepreneurs, with grants of up to $50,000 each. One of the partners in the consortium is the six-year-old Canadian Women's Foundation, which offers its own set of grants to women starting up community-based businesses in remote and rural locations across the country. (For contact information on both groups, see pages 238 and 239.)

JUGGLING FOR YOUR LIFE

What drives many women out of "traditional" jobs, and often into business for themselves, is the perpetual conflict between the kinds of work we do: what we do for money, status, and security versus what we do for health, comfort, and love. Of course, love can often be found on both sides of the equation, which is what turns this conflict into a true dilemma. You love your work, you love your family, but the day is too short, and you can't do it all. This is where the "life balancing" experts are supposed to come in — but as everyone who has taken such a course knows all too well, there's no magic formula that allows you to truly do (or have) it all. You might be able to get things into balance, and even keep them that way for awhile. But then some crisis comes knocking and the whole fragile structure topples to the ground.

Things started toppling for me in the winter of 1995, about six months before I quit my job. In fact, this is what marked the beginning of the end of my days at the magazine. My daughter had just come down with a nasty case of chickenpox, twelve days after her little sister had been hit by the virus; my husband was out of town; my mother was in hospital with a life-threatening illness; and there I was, scratching the psoriasis that always flares up when I'm stressed and sleep-deprived, and trying to finish my fiscal 1996 worksheets, already two weeks over deadline. My heart, needless to say, was not in those worksheets. Now, if that had been my own company, I'd have fed those sheets through the shredder and walked out the door. Or (a more sane approach) I'd have hired someone to handle them for me, at any cost. But it wasn't my company, so I called in a babysitter for my daughter, swallowed my fears about my mom, yelled at my husband long-distance, salved my psoriasis, and kept working.

At about the same time, I watched a drama unfold within my circle of friends. Gilly, a forty-year-old mother of three young children, had been diagnosed with breast cancer, and Sherry had stepped in to provide daily support, both at home and at the hospital, during Gilly's surgery and the ensuing chemotherapy. Sherry was not working, so she was able to do this. At least, that's how we viewed it at the time (*we* being Gilly's full-time-working friends). If we hadn't been working so hard, we told ourselves, we'd have been there for Gilly, too.

Or would we? Now that I'm no longer "working" in that way, I'm not so inclined to forgive myself. In fact, I can't believe I spent so many years with such a narrow view of the meaning of work. In what way was Sherry "not working" through those long months of support to Gilly? Sherry, too, had a life, if not a full-time job like mine. She had two young children, was a regular volunteer at the local crisis centre, and was studying to become a therapist. Here's the irony: while so-called superwomen like me take credit for our amazing ability to juggle, most of us aren't half as good at it as so-called non-working women like Sherry. While I was basically juggling one very large ball (my job) and routinely whisking the others under a rug, she was keeping three or four big ones up in the air. And she was probably reaping far greater satisfaction.

You might think the difference between Sherry and me is personality — and you'd be partly right. But the larger part is how we've defined ourselves through our work — mine for pay, hers for love. In defining myself as a "working woman," I had reduced everything that wasn't "work" to the lower rank of "personal." Those things I did for love, and for which I was not paid, were *not really work*. Raising children fell into that category, along with making a home, investing in my marriage, taking care of my health, and being there for friends.

This is what the balancing classes teach working women to do: make all those pesky personal balls small enough to fit under the carpet at work, so that

> **Balancing classes teach working women to make all those personal balls small enough to fit under the carpet at work . . .**

you can keep that big career ball up in the air. That's why, more often than not, it's your company that sends you out to get balanced, on their tab. Why is it that most of the people sent to these courses are women? And why do they keep getting sent back to take another course, and another? Is it that we're failures in the balancing department? Or does someone have his thumb on the scales?

Most women, in fact, are extremely skilled at juggling, and can do so with grace and good cheer — given permission to juggle and a reasonable selection of balls. Unfortunately, in our male-culture careers, we don't usually get that kind of permission. We are handed the one very large ball, and are expected to ignore the rest — or to toss them off to other women who are not as *gain*fully employed. The result is debilitating stress — and, despite what everyone tells you, this is not due to juggling. Juggling may tire women, but what really stresses them is *not* juggling: not having the *permission* to juggle all those terribly important parts of their lives.

Psychologists make a crucial distinction between stress and undue stress. We all have stress, and some say we need it as fuel for a productive life. *Undue* stress is the toxic stress, the stress that arises when we're forced to give up the goals and ideals that feed us, in the service of someone else's goals and ideals. A job that consumes all of your time and energy without meeting your own goals or ideals presents just that kind of emotional tyranny. Similarly, a job that meets only one goal or ideal while consuming all of your time and energy causes undue stress for women, much more than for men, because we're cut from a different cloth. We need more diversity in our lives.

The classic male "provider" role is too narrow for a lot of women, which is why the jobs that go with it cause us such grief. They cause grief for a lot of men, too — but that's another book. The culprit is not work, but what has been defined as the *male model of working* — a distinction that your husband or partner may not understand at first. When you say you want to quit a job, he might hear *I want to quit working*, when what you really want is to start working differently: to do *more*, not less.

It took me a long time to understand this distinction — to see that I didn't want to stop working, I just wanted to start working more diversely. My all-or-nothing job had robbed me of the opportunity to live a rich and diverse life in which other jobs — the for-love jobs of nurturing, supporting, reaching out, creating relationships and feeding them — could be given their due time and place. It's not that I had abdicated my duties on all those fronts. In fact, I had been doing many of those for-love jobs all along, but I was cramming them into the precious few moments at the end of my workday. I was, in other words, way out of balance. This would explain the fantasies I entertained in the last years of my job — visions of myself living in a hut somewhere in the mountains doing, at most, one thing. Knitting a sweater, or less: watching the sun travel across the sky. Of course, once I quit and passed through the decompression stage, my natural sense of balance re-emerged and I was ready to start working again: doing *more*, not less. This past year has been the busiest and most varied of my life, not to mention one of the happiest. According to psychologist Brunetta Wolfman, my experience is a typical one.

"Many women I have interviewed could not ever remember 'doing nothing,' " writes Wolfman in a recent study. (She is a therapist and teacher at the Stone Center for Developmental Services and Studies at Wellesley, Massachusetts.)

> They had always been busy and active, and their level of activity increased as they got older. With each increase of activity, women became more and more proficient at handling many responsibilities, moving from role to role with ease, without excessive stress. In fact, when I asked hundreds of women how or when they began a pattern of carrying on lots of activities, most of them had difficulty in remembering. When they began to examine their lives, they realized that they had learned, with family encouragement — from parents and grandparents, from examples in their home circle and neighborhood — watching what women did.*

There are some radical implications here for our concept of choice. Many of us think we have to choose — between work and family, between our public and private lives. Wolfman and many other therapists who work with women are saying that choice is not the issue; *being whole* is the issue. If I am faced with making a choice between important aspects of my life, it's best not to take that leap — to back away from the ledge, think it through, consider the possibility of compromise. No single piece of business will suffice as my "best work" — not my job, my family, my friends, or my community. The truth is that my best work includes all of these.

"What concerns me is that we need not say that a woman has to choose between pursuing a career or caring for a family," writes Wolfman in the summary to her study. "That notion is an exaggeration and not a valid concept for women to use as a guide for their lives. Women do not need to and should not give up the diversity which is possible for them."

---

*Reprinted with permission from *Women and Their Many Roles, Work in Progress, No. 7:* obtainable from Stone Center Publications Office, Wellesley College, Wellesley, MA, 02181

THE ART OF COMPROMISE

While Wolfman insists we should not compromise in our quest for diversity, a diverse life suggests its own necessary compromises. All-or-nothing work makes no such demands, and is therefore much easier to do. You just do the job and let everything else suffer.

Back in the days when men were the breadwinners and women the supporters, all-or-nothing work was sustainable. It might not have been healthy, but it was doable, because most of those hard-working men had wives at home to mitigate the suffering. Today, breadwinning is shared and compromise is everywhere — which is a good thing, as far as women are concerned. (Not all men agree.) Even the most successful breadwinning women find times and places for compromise, though it's rarely in the best interests of their careers. The vice-president of a bank, if she is a woman, will feel an irresistible tug of loyalty to a friend whose parent has died, and if she is a good friend and a skilled compromiser, she will find a way to go to her. The provincial court judge, if she is a mom, will understand the importance of volunteering at her child's pre-school at least a couple of times in a year — just like the "non-working" moms do. If her child has a father who is willing and able to do the same, that's a bonus, not an out. These relationship "jobs" are essential work for all of us, and those who are conscientious — those who strive to be whole — will bend over backwards to schedule their *other* jobs around them. To juggle, in other words.

> **A move that demonstrates an increased focus on personal life suggests (to boss and colleagues) a decreased focus on work.**

Striving to be whole is our birthright, says author and child-rights advocate Penelope Leach, and expressing it becomes most challenging, and most important, with the birth of a child. "To suggest that a woman choose between her relationship with her child and her individual adult identity, largely vested in her salary- or wage-earning role, is as idiotic as asking her to choose between food and drink," Leach writes in her 1994 book, *Children First*.

It is not only that both are essential to her, it is also that they are inseparable because they are both part of her. But to suggest that she cannot fulfill the role of mother (or worker) unless she is with her child (or at her desk) seven (or five) days a week is equally idiotic. A musician is not less a musician because he is a civil servant all week, nor less valuable as a civil servant because he spends his weekends in concert halls. A daughter is not less a daughter because she marries nor less a wife because she is also a teacher. Only flexible integration and sequencing of people's various roles can defuse the conflict between parenthood and paid work.*

To integrate our lives and defuse this conflict, we need to find ways to work less. Or at least to put a little less of ourselves into our work so that a little more is left over at the end of the day. This doesn't sound so difficult, especially considering that many of the "non-standard" work arrangements of a few years ago are becoming quite standard today: flex time, work-from-home, compressed work weeks and part-time options are now available to many employees. But such options are not everyone's idea of a compromise worth making. For ambitious women, a move that demonstrates an increased focus on personal life suggests (to boss and colleagues) a decreased focus on work. Working less is *no* way to climb a ladder. And for women in financial hardship, well, you can't downsize when you're already down. At the lower end of the payroll, most women accept the status quo because they don't believe they have much choice. They work the hours they're given, and catch the ball they're thrown. Either that, or they risk being tossed out. And then where are they? In very dire straits, where they can't even feed their children, never mind volunteer at their pre-school.

Without doubt, a great number of women not only *feel* trapped by their jobs; they *are* trapped. Usually, it's financial. As much as they might want to work less, these women — many of them single moms

*From *Children First* by Penelope Leach, ©1994 by Penelope Leach; reprinted by permission of Alfred A. Knopf, Inc.

— can't afford to earn less. But there is one small *can*, and I'll say it at the risk of being called a Pollyanna. We can think about change, even if we can't necessarily make it today. We can look for a better work situation, even if we can't get to it this year. And if we're careful about it, looking won't do us any harm. In fact, it will likely do a world of good, because it forces us to notice things we might otherwise miss: like the fact that many other women in our workplace feel the same way, and that there might be something we can do about it, as a group, without compromising ourselves right out of our jobs. This is how workplaces change, in response to the changing needs and expectations of their workers. One thing we can be sure of is that our workplaces won't change to accommodate our needs if we don't somehow find a way to voice those needs.

FINDING OUR VOICE

Business is by nature a conservative environment, and without pressure to change, it will not change. The employee puts that pressure on, and she does it by making herself valuable. Invaluable, if that's possible. We've all seen what happens when an outstanding employee has a problem at work: Her boss gets busy and helps her solve the problem, making everyone happy in the bargain. That's how rule books get rewritten, and ceilings raised. If one invaluable employee can successfully rewrite the rules for herself, just think what ten or a hundred invaluable employees can accomplish when they put their minds and voices together.

Making myself invaluable at work is a tall order, particularly if I'm dissatisfied with my job. But that's what it takes to bring changes and, with those changes, a new level of personal satisfaction. "Always make the most of your current work situation," advises Barbara Moses in her book *Career Intelligence*. Use the job you've got to make it better, and to make yourself a better candidate for the next job. There are no short cuts; what's called for is an intense focus on positive outcomes, and a liberation from energy-diffusing *victim* behaviour — the scourge of the work world. Victim behaviour is not the same as laziness, but it nets the same deadbeat results: weak focus, low energy, no progress. You could say that allowing yourself to be demoralized by the limitations of a job is tantamount to endorsing those limitations. The deadbeat employee is applying no pressure for change. So here's your choice: You can be a radical, or you can be a deadbeat. (Take the Deadbeat Challenge, page 98.)

Regardless of the power one woman may or may not have to change her work situation today, she does ultimately hold the power to set her own priorities, to plan for tomorrow, and to give voice to her right to juggle all the important things in her life. Doing so will strengthen not only her as an individual, but all working women, in that it joins a collective protest against the status-quo assumption that the value of our work lies only in our pay cheques. A job does not give us licence to shun the essential work that lies beyond the office door. Nor does a job contract give our employers the power to diminish the value of our life's work. Most of us know this, but few of us gather the courage to give voice to it. Some of our colleagues, and many of our employers, will not care to hear this message, but they're going to have to get used to it if enough of us decide that's the way it's going to be — that we are working to live, *not* living to work.

This is starting to sound very much like a movement, and I suppose it is: an evolution of the women's movement that empowers us to live whole lives, to resist labels, and to express fully the rights our mothers and sisters fought so hard to win. The best way to gather strength is to become better informed, and fortunately there is an abundance of resources for women who want to make changes in their work and their workplace. The Radcliffe Public Policy Institute is one such resource, and here is a checklist they've published as part of their "New Economic Equation" — a progressive model for the rebuilding of our economy through the integration of work, family, and community. Browse the list below, and see how your workplace measures up. Discuss your thoughts with your co-workers and colleagues, and consider what role you might play in bringing about change.

Radcliffe Public Policy Institute's New Economic Equation

1. Does your workplace offer all employees of the organization a livable wage that enables them to meet the physical and educational needs of their families?

2. Does your workplace provide opportunities for employee participation through unions or other independently-elected representatives?

3. Does your workplace offer paid or unpaid family leave policies to enable all employees, men and women, to care for children, elderly relatives and/or disabled spouses?

4. Does your workplace offer flexible schedules that help all employees meet outside responsibilities?

5. Does your workplace provide opportunities for employees at all levels of the organization to participate in community activities?

6. Does your workplace allow all employees to have access to portable health insurance and retirement plans?

7. Does your workplace provide educational and training programs to allow each worker to develop and maintain knowledge and skills essential for the changing economy?

8. Does your workplace offer attractive alternatives to full-time jobs — such as job-sharing, reduced hours, or working from home — that come with benefits and options for promotion?

9. Does your workplace provide an environment that is safe and secure and free from discrimination for all employees?

10. Does your workplace encourage people at all levels of the organization to put into action work-family-community policies?

EX-FILE | *Bureaucrat in Limbo*

NAME: Anne Mauch, 42

EX: Strategic planning director

CURRENT: In transition

RÉSUMÉ HIGHLIGHTS: Degrees in forestry and economics; worked as a forester; joined federal department of Western Economic Diversification in 1987, later appointed director of Edmonton office, $75,000 salary and staff of ten; business events manager at Asia Pacific Economic Cooperation Forum, Vancouver, 1997.

PERSONAL: Single

BACKGROUND: A year and a half ago, when I was at Economic Diversification, I applied for a job. It was a promotion that I was supposed to apply for, that I was lined up for. Everyone knew it was "my job" — that I would get it. It was the next step on the ladder, a move to a larger office with a bigger staff. And I did get it, but on the day they were set to announce it, I changed my mind and turned it down.

The problem was not just that particular job. I suddenly started questioning the process of continually applying for the next job, of always needing to be moving up every few years — I mean, what was I getting out of this? As soon as I get this job, I'll be thinking well, what's the next job or what's the next promotion or the next expectation. I was in a trap. I got a lot out of what I did, and enjoyed most of it, but I was dying to do something completely different, unexpected.

ON MENTORS AND MEN: I think a large part of the problem was I haven't seen very many positive role models of senior women with the federal government. I think they pay a huge,

huge price to get where they are. Their whole life revolves around their work. Most of the women senior to me were not married, which allowed them to be defined by their work. They may have friends and other interests, but there's a hollowness. I'm not married either, but I guess I'm not prepared to define myself as being the senior person in an organization. I mean, so what? In the end, that's all I could say about the prospect of my own promotion. So what? Maybe to a few people in the department I'm going to be a little more important. I'm going to have a bigger staff, make a little more money. But I'll be putting in more hours — I was already working ten-hour days and many weekends — and there'll be more personnel problems, and lots more office politics — and for what?

At first, I thought I could just turn down the promotion and stay at my job. I thought I could try to do my job differently — resisting that automatic reflex of moving up to the next level. But that's easier said than done. I found when I turned down the promotion, I was sidelined; I was no longer in that group of people who were going somewhere. And that was disappointing, not just to me but to some of the more senior women who thought they were grooming me. One of them said to me, "Do you know what you're doing? You haven't just turned down a promotion. You've put yourself on the line. Don't expect anything else from us." I was terrified.

Playing amateur psychologist, I'd say I offended those women because I wasn't making the same choice they'd made. Most of them looked at me like, "What's the matter with you?" But there were a few who probably felt, well, I wish I had been able to make such a choice.

Men don't seem to be so conflicted. The ones I've worked with seem much clearer about how and why they work, which is probably because most of them have a female support system called a wife. Even if their wife works, she still tends to be the person responsible for everything else in their lives. We women used to joke about how we needed a wife, too. But you know, that wouldn't have solved the problem for me. I'd probably have treated my wife the way a lot of men treat theirs. Maybe I'm not being fair to men, but I'm not sure men who rely on their wives to support them end up having very rich lives. Most men seem to want different things than women do — I didn't really want someone at home cooking dinner for me. I'd want someone to cook dinner *with*.

There's a perception that it's easier for single women to move up in their careers, because they only have *themselves* to worry about, and to some degree maybe that's true. But the single person still has family, and friends, and other interests, and all these are diminished when you focus too much on your job. In a way, women who have husbands and children are forced to live a more balanced life than those of us who are single. They have to go home for dinner. They have to make family time on weekends.

THE TRANSITION: Ultimately, I can only say what's best for me, and I have to take responsibility for my choices. My job didn't limit me. I limited myself, because I chose to give so much of myself to my work and put so much emphasis on that. Like a lot of people, I got so far into it that I forgot it was a choice. Turning down that promotion suddenly opened up a lot of other choices. I realized there was a lot more than just the promotion that I needed to figure out. So I spent time thinking, and reading, and talking to my friends.

What I realized was that more than anything I wanted to improve the quality of my relationships with friends and family, and to live closer to my mom. I've managed to keep up relationships over the years, but haven't been able to give the kind of depth to them that I would like. I'd like to spend more time at home. I like gardening. I like cooking, but for years there's been a lot of why-bother meals: eating out of the fridge, or picking up something on my way home.

The fact that I was approaching my fortieth birthday probably had a lot to do with it. When you're young, you're proving yourself. Then you hit the stage where you've shown you can "do it" and now you can choose not to. Maybe I wouldn't have figured all this out if I hadn't been offered that promotion. The promotion confirmed for me that I was able to take the next step — and allowed me to say no to it. I don't need to prove anything any more. My younger female friends still have a lot to prove, so they can't relate to this at all — to the idea that your life isn't necessarily one long, straight line leading to bigger and better jobs.

I took a leave of absence and moved to Vancouver to spend some time with my mom. When the APEC job came up, it was the perfect opportunity. It was a one-year secondment from Economic Diversification, to manage APEC's business events and sponsorships. I was able to get out of my old work environment for a year, and think about my future with a clean slate — while being paid for it. I was really lucky. It allowed me to make connections and start to see new employment opportunities, and it helped me to finalize my decision not to go back to my old job. I have to constantly guard myself, though, against jumping right into the next job. I'm trying really hard to keep myself open, and to think long term. We're so programmed to solve the problem, make the decision. I still have a lot of exploring to do.

THE NEW MENTOR: Living with my mom has been really interesting. She's spent her whole life at home, but she manages to keep herself fully occupied and just as productive as the women I've worked with, just in different ways. At home, there's always something to do. Being around her, I've discovered a new sense of rhythm — of working around the home, gardening and cooking and fixing up the house. She doesn't drive, so I'm the wheels in the family. I've made my life revolve around her, and it's been fun, maybe in part because we're so different. My mom is very Old World. I've never seen her in a pair of pants. She gardens in a dress.

I guess she's my new mentor. It's odd but we're in a similar situation, and we're able to help each other. She's in transition too — living in this house by herself since my dad died, not knowing when to leave and where to go. Neither of us are really sure where we're going, but we're both a lot more comfortable with being unsure than we were a year ago, so I guess that's progress —being able to leave things open and not get distressed by that.

EX-FILE | *The World Changer*

NAME: Sheila Fruman, 48

EX: Communications director, Premier's Office

CURRENT: Consultant; media commentator

RÉSUMÉ HIGHLIGHTS: BA, MA Communications; Media relations, BC Daycare Action Coalition (unpaid), 1983–85; Education/Communication Director, Legal Services Society of BC, 1979–86; Communications Director, BC Government Employees Union, 1986–91; Director of Strategic Planning, Premier's Office, 1991–93; Communications Director, Premier's Office, 1993–95.

PERSONAL: Divorced; one daughter, Roseanna, 15.

BACKGROUND: For almost twenty-five years I put my work above everything else in my life. I'm not sure it was conscious, but looking back now it is so obvious. My work defined me. I didn't even like vacations that much because without my work I really had no idea who I was. I felt uncomfortable without the daily props to remind me of my "identity" and what I should be doing. In hindsight I realize that almost every time I changed my job, I changed the man in my life, too. Either he was involved with my work, or there was just no room for him.

I don't know exactly where this work obsession came from, but I'm sure it started very early. I always knew I would work, probably because I was aware of my own mother's frustration as a housewife. I concluded her unhappiness came from wanting to do more with her life, and I was hell-bent that I would, even if she didn't. I was fortunate that my parents gave me a university education and when I graduated I was determined to "change the world." I never thought of this — changing the world — in terms of a career, but twenty-five years later it's obvious I made it one.

WHY I QUIT: The most difficult period was in 1993 to '95, when I was Communications Director for Mike Harcourt. I was living in Vancouver, working in Victoria, and was the mother of a pre-teen daughter who lived with her father while I was out of town. Coming home Thursday night was like arriving at a deserted motel — empty fridge, empty cupboards, empty feeling. It was as if no one lived there. Roseanna would come to stay at my place but I felt like I had missed the routine of the school week. Often, I was so exhausted I spent most of the weekend recovering from the week's events. By the time I had the house warmed up, a few groceries on the shelf, and had sorted through the stack of mail and bills that had piled up during the week, it was time to take off again.

Twelve-hour work days were routine, especially because I had nothing to go home for in Victoria. My three nights a week there were spent at a friend's house where I envied the fact she got to live and work in the same place. Even though we kept in daily contact, I missed seeing my daughter and felt torn between my work and the rest of my life.

THE TURNING POINT: In the summer of 1994 a vicious power struggle developed in the Premier's Office between his two top advisors. I was caught in the middle of it. Although I was reassured by the Premier that things would be resolved, an increasing amount of my time was taken up by the games being played — so much time, in fact, that I felt my work was losing its value.

I had proven I could play the game as well as the boys, but that didn't give me any kind of satisfaction. When I realized that the only way to stay in the job was to continue to play a game that didn't interest me — one that was preventing me from doing the work I loved and undermining my integrity and self-respect — I realized I had to quit. For so many years the stimulation and sense of accomplishment at work seemed to justify the constant struggle to balance work and my personal life. But towards the end, it wasn't worth the price I was paying either at work or in the rest of my life. This was especially hard to accept considering how committed I was to my work and the value I placed on making a meaningful contribution in the world.

TAKE-OUT WISDOM: I'm grateful for the opportunities I've had to work, learn from my experience and, hopefully, make a contribution to my community. There's no question it has been demanding and maybe I would have done things differently if I knew when I first started out what I know now. Thank God I had a daughter somewhere along the way and even though it's been hard, I've managed to develop a close relationship with her. Since I've quit my job I especially enjoy the ease of taking her to the doctor or picking her up from a dance class or just being there when she feels like talking. I still feel strongly that work is important, but it's not everything. As women, maybe we overreacted to the challenges and new opportunities available to us without thinking through the options. I still wonder if there were alternatives that would have been satisfying on all fronts.

NEXT: Now that I've "made it" in the conventional world, I want to find a way of "making it" on my own terms. I'm not sure yet what that means but I'm having fun figuring it out. Meanwhile, I'm spending lots of time at home and with friends. I'm here for my daughter when she needs me and I've made our relationship a priority.

It was scary letting go of a high-profile position. At first I feared I would be invisible, but now I feel I'm more *me* than I've ever been. I really doubt that I would jump back into the kind of all-or-nothing jobs I used to have — there seem to be so many other options to do meaningful work and have a fuller life.

 **CHECK** |
| *Your Prospects for Success*

1. **TAKE THE DEADBEAT CHALLENGE**

   Take this challenge to determine whether you're on your way to invaluability at work, or on your way nowhere, fast. Circle A or B for each of the following:

	AGREE	DISAGREE
I spend a lot of work time thinking about not being there.	B	A
I spend a lot of home time thinking about my work.	A	B
I am more comfortable staying with routine work than taking on a difficult new task.	B	A

	AGREE	DISAGREE
If I have time to spare at work, I relax at my desk but try to look busy.	B	A
My work fulfils many of my needs for challenge and excitement.	A	B
Money is the main reason I'm staying in this job.	B	A
I start most days feeling positive about what I can achieve.	A	B
I enjoy the experience of going through a performance appraisal, and will ask for one if it's overdue.	A	B
There are qualities I admire in most of my superiors.	A	B
I would apply for an exciting promotion even if I had doubts about my qualification.	A	B
I can tell you what my job description says without having to look it up.	A	B
I've taken vocation-related training in the past year.	A	B
I enjoy talking to co-workers about shared problems.	B	A

How did you score? What does it mean?

SEVEN OR MORE Bs: You score high on the deadbeat scale, which doesn't necessarily mean *you're* the deadbeat. It could be your employer who's got the bad attitude, and all that negativity is catching. In that case, you might be better off working somewhere else. But think carefully before shifting blame. With such a high B-score, there's got to be some attitude deficit on both sides. Major adjustments are called for.

BETWEEN FIVE AND SEVEN Bs: You're a situational dead-beat, which means there's hope — if faint. What you need is a shot of psychic energy to help you overcome your resistance to change. Start by writing your own mission statement (see page 131) to evaluate how well your current job fits into your life's mission. If the shoe basically fits but is pinching a couple of toes, focus on making those fine adjustments.

BETWEEN THREE AND FIVE Bs: You're close to average on the deadbeat scale, which means you're a lousy deadbeat and a pretty valuable employee. These days, however, *pretty* valuable won't take you far. If you're just treading water at work and sat-isfied with that for now, relax and keep treading. There are times in our lives when that's all we can expect from a job. If, on the other hand, you're ready for more challenge, think about how you can juice up your own engines. Take a course. Start a club. Use your Rolodex.

TWO Bs OR LESS: Welcome to value-land. You've got the right attitude — but are you seeing the right results? If not, you might be the proverbial square peg in a round hole. Go job shopping. Or stay where you are, but look for ways to channel some of that positive energy into pressing your employer for change.

2. ARE YOU A WORKAHOLIC?

A culture that puts too much value on our work — much more than it puts on our families, our communities, our bodies, our souls — is fertile ground for the disease of workaholism. In a 1997 article in the *New York Times Magazine*, Arlie Russell Hochschild reports on a study she conducted of three thousand parents whose children attended day-care centres. One-third of fathers and one-fifth of mothers described themselves as workaholic, and one out of three said their partners were.

Obviously, many of us recognize we're victims of workaholism, but we shrug it off because it doesn't seem all that serious. It strikes us as a healthier condition than laziness — and it certainly pays better. Or so we think, until we succumb to the terminal stages.

This quiz will help you decide whether you are overconscientious or undermotivated when it comes to work. Circle A or B for each of the following:

	AGREE	DISAGREE
Suffering for your job is not positive.	A	B
I need to make more sacrifices to succeed in my career.	B	A
More leisure time will make us a better society.	A	B
If you want a job done well it's better to do it yourself.	B	A
People may not succeed no matter how hard they work.	A	B
I respect self-made people more than others.	B	A
How good I feel about myself does not depend on work.	A	B
Competition is good for you.	B	A
There is no point to doing unpaid overtime.	A	B
I feel uneasy if there is little work to do.	B	A

How did you score? What does it mean?

SEVEN OR MORE Bs: You score high on the workaholic scale. You could be putting your health and relationships at risk and may well benefit from counselling. You need to learn to relax. Put work in perspective and try sleeping late on the weekend.

BETWEEN FIVE AND SEVEN Bs: You are not as obsessively hard-working as higher scorers but you are scoring above average in having a positive attitude to hard work. You probably don't have a problem, but make sure you aren't working extra hours just for the sake of it.

BETWEEN THREE AND FIVE Bs: You score around or a little below the average on valuing hard work, so your problem is not so much working too hard, it's more a question of not taking your work seriously enough! This doesn't mean you are not a hard worker, but you are too tolerant of laziness and make more excuses for it than you should.

TWO Bs OR LESS: You score very low in valuing hard work and this is partly because you have great difficulty conforming to what society regards as appropriate behaviour. Your success in life is more likely to come from inspiration than from hard slog.

Reprinted from the Daily Mail.

FOUR

The Mother of
All Conflicts

THAT WAS THEN	THIS IS NOW
Busy	Full
Free from children	Free for children
Quality time	Quantity time
Have it all	Have a life
Nouveau riche	Nouveau pauvre
The risk of compromise	The joy of compromise
Sexual revolution	Kitchen-table revolution
Correct choice	My choice
Stay at home	Work at home

If the new liberation means freedom to juggle, then this question remains: Why do so many women, and working mothers in particular, complain constantly and bitterly about all the juggling they have to do? And what was my own multitasking problem if not a case of juggler's fatigue? The last chapter touched on an answer, and this chapter will delve deeper. What I needed was to make a crucial distinction between a full life and a just plain busy life. To achieve fullness and something close to balance (perfect balance is a pipe dream),

I had to make time and space for the essential parts of my life, and find a nice back burner on which to store the rest. The real challenge was deciding what "essential" meant to me.

This is what I've learned since quitting: that there was nothing wrong with my multitasking approach to life, but there was plenty wrong with the way I lined up my tasks. Or, more accurately, the way I failed to line them up. My main problem was having one of those all-or-nothing jobs, which I loved and wanted to be a success at. I also had some stubborn notions (all of them time-consuming) about how to raise my children and how to be a good wife, doting daughter, loving sister, and trusty friend, not to mention a willing volunteer, fitness buff, and lifelong learner. Trying to be all things to all people only served to obscure my own sense of self, and it handicapped me as a juggler because I was being tossed along with the balls.

THE CHICKEN-SOUP CHALLENGE

Defining "essential" for oneself is a tough assignment (there's an exercise at the end of this chapter to help you define yours). Few of us are immune to the ways in which our families, friends, employers, mentors, ministers, policy makers, and even TV talk-show hosts dictate what is and what isn't essential. My good friend Karen Gelman, the globe-trotting oncologist from the Girls' Night Out gang, rose to the challenge in a recent late-night phone call, the two of us blabbing quietly in our darkened houses at two ends of the city, husbands and children all long asleep. "It's different for everyone," said my insomniac friend, who works harder than anyone I know. At forty-four, she is constantly torn between caring for her two young daughters and for her clinic full of breast-cancer patients, but she has never for a minute considered easing up on her workload, nor would anyone want her to. Torn is simply a way of life for her. "I love my job," she says. "And I've made my choices: I just don't bother to make chicken soup from scratch."

Neither of us laughed. We both recognized in her confession a difficult, well-reasoned response to an onslaught of conflicting pressures, not the least of which was the weight of the centuries-old tradition passed from Jewish mother to Jewish daughter concerning the laborious preparation of a "proper" Friday night dinner. Karen had decided in her wisdom that packaged soup was proper enough for her.

My own downfall as a multitasker had its chicken-soup dimension. Friday afternoons regularly found me in a funk at my desk, itching to be home, to be *making* a home, preparing for the most important meal of the week. At least, it had been the most important meal of the week when I was growing up. In my parents' house, the Sabbath was welcomed in a mood I can only describe as sweet exhaustion mingled with gratitude: exhaustion from a week of work, study, stress, and sheer busy-ness; gratitude for our good fortune in having this family, this home, this beautiful table lit by Shabbat candles and infused with the aroma of real chicken soup (my mom made *the* best). Friday night dinner was the week's reward, and the start of a much-needed day of repose — from sundown Friday to Saturday's first star. No matter what was on our social calendars — and as my two sisters and I grew to adolescence, we had no shortage of opportunities to be out with friends — our attendance was always required at Friday dinner, and we obliged, if not always with a smile. We understood that this was the symbolic underpinning of our family life, and before it, all scheduling conflicts dissolved like salt in the broth.

How differently life evolved for my young family. Even when I managed to sneak out of the office by four on a Friday afternoon, racing home with take-out chicken, canned broth, and a bakery pie, I could not come close to creating the Shabbat feeling by sundown. At best, I created a mock-Shabbat feeling: we sang the blessings and slurped the soup, but the kids knew that after dinner their dad would disappear into his office with his week-ahead planner and I would be snapping mad if they didn't help clean up and "please go to bed quietly because Mommy is very, very tired." Sometimes, we didn't even light the candles. What kind of symbolism was I creating here for my children? What kind of home?

I might have solved this conflict by leaving work earlier on Fridays, or by "doing Shabbat" on Saturdays instead. But I was too busy being busy to figure this out. I wasn't looking for solutions, because I didn't understand what the problem was.

Oh, I knew I was too busy, but wasn't everybody? My conflict was no worse than that of most working moms. Nor was my Friday crunch much different from my Monday-to-Thursday crunch, when you got right down to it. And they both paled in comparison to the *real* crunch of summer: the kids having been sprung from school only to find themselves restructured into non-stop activities that would distract them and us from the promise of freedom that summer vacation should have spelled. I had little choice about this, as long as I remained editor-in-chief of the magazine, because (like most magazines) we made our entire year's profit in the fall season, which meant full-out production from June through October. I certainly couldn't give myself more time off than I gave my staff, and the summer vacation rule was two weeks maximum — or we'd never get those big fall issues out the door.

In fact, one of the first things I did on taking over as editor-in-chief was to push the maximum from one to two weeks. A week's vacation was an insult, almost worse than no vacation at all. On the other hand, my taking two weeks off during the busiest production period of the year meant several days of panicky preparation for the escape, followed by an overflowing in-tray on returning to work. On balance, vacations were hardly worth it — except for those precious moments of family time in between the crunches. I savoured those moments, and tried not to think about the rest.

Where working motherhood is concerned, it's often best not to think too much. Better to just keep working because, well, what's the alternative? Stepping back at work? Taking a *smaller* job — one that could be done *part-time*? Putting your career on pause, if not into serious jeopardy, after all those years of beavering your way up the ladder? Yes, there are alternatives, but they're hardly attractive for women or men to whom career advancement is essential. For ambitious workers, family-friendly *alternatives* read like career-threatening *compromises*. To find time for family, you have to take it from work. We all know now that the old saw about quality time was a bad joke made up by some guy in personnel. Your family needs *quantity* time, just as your employer does, so it's your choice. And the more passion and promise you've invested in your career, the tougher it is to choose family.

That explains why, even at workplaces that are family friendly, relatively few employees actually make use of options such as flex or part-time. A study of 188 American companies, conducted by the Families and Work Institute a few years ago, found that 35 per cent of those companies offered a work-from-home option, but fewer than 3 per cent of their employees took advantage of it. And while a majority of companies in the study offered part-time shifts, fewer than 5 per cent of their employees opted for them. Pulling back from full-time, full-out work simply goes against the grain. It threatens our financial security, but, even more than that, it represents a kind of defeat — an admission that our families count at least as much as our jobs, which for a lot of men and women feels like the first step on a slippery career slope.

For ambitious workers, family-friendly *alternatives* read like career-threatening *compromises*. To find time for family, you have to take it from work.

That your family can be poison to your career has long been understood by feminists. Half a century ago, Simone de Beauvoir wrote, "No woman should be authorized to stay at home to raise her children. Women should not have that choice, precisely because if there is such a choice, too many women will make that one." And so feminists embraced day care as the antidote, and it worked. But as it turned out, it only cures a symptom, not the disease that is systemic in our work culture. Having our kids taken care of doesn't ease the inhuman pace of the managerial career path, the emphasis on "face time" as a measure of dedication to the job, or the male bias that starts in the boardroom and trickles down. Notes Patricia Schroeder, a former US congresswoman: "It's easier to take time off from work to get a car fixed than to take time off to look after our families."

"If you want to have children, proceed at your own risk," warns Betsy Morris in her March 1997 cover story for *Fortune* magazine, titled "Is Your Family Wrecking Your Career?" "You must be very talented, or on very solid ground, to overcome the damage a family can do to your career." Morris points to a 1995 survey at Eli Lilly & Co. in which just 36 per cent of workers said it was possible to get ahead and still devote sufficient time to their families (and Lilly has a reputation as one of America's most family-friendly companies). Similar results were reported in a 1996 study by Carleton University professor Linda Duxbury. Surveying 27,000 workers across Canada, she found that parental leave is widely considered detrimental to one's career, which is why less than 1 per cent of fathers actually take it. Success is still very much defined by being there, full-time.

All of which helps to explain why we're such a deeply conflicted generation of women — and so very prone to feeling guilty. Guilty that we're not able to focus on our jobs as well as we think we ought to, *and* guilty that we're short-changing our children by trying. What a pity that we can't see, when we're in the midst of it, that this insanity springs from a small error in judgement — a misinterpretation of those two words, "great things." How often do we find ourselves willing to sacrifice great things at home to achieve not-so-great things at work? We do this every day, when we are working for the rewards of competition — for status, excitement, challenge, wealth. This is how we "make our name," or so our competitive society teaches us. But what is all that for, if not to make life better for ourselves and for society?

Shirley Burggraf, author of the 1997 book *The Feminine Economy and Economic Man*, says "a great moral awakening" is in store, to correct the notion that what happens at home is somehow less important than what happens on the job. Strong, progressive-minded women will herald that awakening — women who are weary of living on either side of the line we have carved, that very deep gorge between the world where people compete and the world where they care. "In a world in which people are free to choose between caring and competitive roles," writes Burggraf, "an economic system that disproportionately rewards the competitors and beggars the caretakers will eventually lose its ability to compete because resources are increasingly diverted away from society's basic function of providing a civilized context for human life." We need to divert some of those precious resources back to the task of bringing up well-loved, wise, and caring children. That, after all, is one of our best opportunities for greatness.

WHAT KIND OF MOTHERS ARE WE?

Sheila Fruman, the subject of the Ex-File on page 95, told me it took her more than two decades of work to see that her success was built in part on what she saw as her mother's failings. It was almost as though the rage she felt about her mother's housebound life propelled Fruman to live a house-free life, as far as possible from baby food and vacuum cleaners. At the age of forty-six, reality hit. The work in which she'd invested everything was failing to reward her in kind. She was earning points in a high-stakes game, but points could not feed her growing hunger for deeper meaning, for real connection. It suddenly occurred to her that although she had always thought she "loved" her work, this was nothing like the love she felt for her daughter, half of whose young life she had missed because she'd been working so hard. "I had thrown the baby out with the bathwater," she told me over a cup of tea, blinking the tears away. Fortunately, it wasn't too late to go and get that baby back, and to rebuild a nest and a modest career around her.

My chicken-soup mania came from the same emotional hunger as Fruman's, though mine was milder. It helped that my job didn't take me away from my family nearly as much as Fruman's did, nor did my marriage break down as a result of the stress, as hers had. Her job forced her to choose between a home life and a work life — an easy choice given her resolve to do things differently from her mother. I never made such a clear choice, perhaps because part of me pined for my mom's less complicated life. Instead of suffering the collision of two worlds, I suffered the fatigue of living in both at once. I didn't so much reject my mother's world as try to combine it with my father's. So, while I did throw out the bathwater, I never tossed the babies.

As my professional savvy and pride swelled, I never lost my need for home-made emotional nourishment. I never believed that home-love could be replaced by work-love, though life would have been a lot less complicated if it could. Living in two worlds *is* complicated. It does not promote the kind of focus a person needs to climb and to sustain position at work. Sheila Fruman was far better equipped than I to break through the glass ceiling. On the other hand, she was probably bruised more deeply than I when she fell off her ladder. In the end, neither of us "successful" working moms were entirely proud of what we'd achieved.

This is what Elizabeth Fox-Genovese means when she says that for today's women, "the problem that has no name" is children. For 1960s housewives, according to Betty Friedan, the problem was the terrible frustration of being cut off from the larger world for which their college education had prepared them. The ensuing thirty years, thanks in part to Friedan and her revolutionary colleagues, have brought countless opportunities for women to channel their talents and energies into economic, political, and social achievement at every level. Yet we have still not achieved true equality with men, as Fox-Genovese points out in her book *Feminism Is Not the Story of My Life*, and lately our energies have started to wane. That's because, for all the freedom we've won, many of us remain as trapped as those 1960s housewives — but instead of being isolated at home by the job of raising children, we're now more likely to be ghettoized into the lower end of the workforce,

> **I didn't so much reject my mother's world as try to combine it with my father's. While I did throw out the bathwater, I never tossed the babies.**

where it is still possible (if just barely) to both work *and* raise children. Some liberation!

Writes Fox-Genovese:

> Children, not men, restrict women's independence. Children, not men, tend to make and keep women poor. Few but the most radical feminists have been willing to state openly that women's freedom requires their freedom from children. Yet the covert determination to free women from children shapes much feminist thought and most feminist policies, even, and especially, those policies aimed at having the government assume a large part of the responsibility. Thus, disagreement about the relation between women and children explodes into the angry cultural war between feminists and conservatives, although many Americans who are not palpably conservative are joining the anti-feminist side.*

At the centre of this confrontation, says Fox-Genovese, lies the question of responsibility for children. Are women responsible, or is society? So here we are, back in the family-values debate, with social democrats backing the feminists in their drive to make society a better guardian to our children, while conservatives insist that parents ought to just buckle down and do their own job better. Mothers, in particular, bear the brunt of the conservatives' wrath. Motherhood is about sacrifice, they say, and we ought to accept this if we care about our kids. To feminists, of course, such rhetoric only serves men's determination to control women and keep them dependent.

> Responding to feminist rhetoric, conservatives argue that feminists intend nothing less than the destruction of the family, and the intimacy and privacy it affords. Those who remain

*From *Feminism Is Not the Story of My Life*, by Elizabeth Fox-Genovese; reprinted by permission of Doubleday, a division of Bantam Doubleday Dell Publishing Group, Inc.

uneasy with both extremes face difficult questions. Are there any differences between women and men that explain why the responsibility for children must fall more heavily on women? If so, how may we protect women's necessary economic independence? May we assume that, in general, children benefit from the focused attention of their own parents or of close family members, and that making it possible for them to enjoy such attention should rank as a national priority? If so, what policies would best serve children's needs, and should they be provided through public or private means? Almost everyone now recognizes the problems, but we cannot agree on solutions, especially if they cost money.

This debate boiled up during the 1996 US presidential campaign, then spilled over into Canada later the same fall when Ontario's Conservative Premier Mike Harris launched a school breakfast program and, with it, a thinly veiled attack on working women. "If you go back thirty or forty years, it seemed to be that mom was in the kitchen with a hot breakfast cooking when everybody woke up in the morning. That's not the normal situation today," said the premier, suggesting that it was somehow the fault of working mothers that his government had to spend money on school breakfasts. Hmm. So, kids are going to school hungry because mom's too busy working to fix them breakfast? And this has nothing to do with the 22 per cent cut in welfare benefits introduced by the Harris government during the preceding two years — cuts affecting about half a million children, many of whose moms are living at home with them, in poverty? Needless to say, Harris caught hell for his comments. "June Cleaver doesn't live on my street, Premier," shouted New Democrat Frances Lankin during the ensuing debate in the legislature. Which prompted Conservative member Joseph Spina to take aim at her: "Go home and take care of your own kids!"

Such extreme positions are exactly the problem, and in this case, both sides are wrong. Just because women work doesn't mean they, or their husbands, can't find the two minutes it takes to fix a decent breakfast for their kids. And just because some women stay home doesn't mean they're doing a good job raising their children. A working woman who is fulfilled at her job and has found some sense of balance can be a much more positive force at home than a bored or depressed, stay-at-home mom.

Not that staying home has to be boring or depressing — which brings me to Frances Lankin's error: June Cleaver *is* alive and well, and living contentedly in almost every neighbourhood on the continent. She's a hockey mom, a ballet mom, a crossing-guard mom, a church-bazaar mom, a PTA mom, a home-schooling mom, and any of the countless other variations of the stay-at-home classic. Aside from the soccer moms, who unwittingly found their voice in the 1996 US presidential campaign, most at-home moms just do their thing quietly and invisibly — which is why Lankin may not have noticed any June Cleavers on her street.

RADICAL MRS. CLEAVER

June Cleaver certainly *does* live on my street. In fact, there are hundreds of June Cleavers in my neck of the suburban woods — though they don't wear high heels and pearls when they vacuum, or dab powder on their noses on their way to greet their kids at the back door with a tray of freshly baked cookies. The at-home moms I've gotten to know since quitting my job are a radicalized version of the Beav's mom. In all, the 1990s Mrs. Cleaver is a much more complex and admirable character. She has decided that if it's okay to do all-or-nothing work in an office, then it's okay to do it at home. That if she can afford to opt out of the conflict-ridden work world where compromise lurks round every corner, why not opt the hell out — and into a simpler life where the children come a clear, uncontested first? Why is it somehow more admirable to compromise my kids, asks today's June Cleaver, than to compromise my career?

Nor are all the new June Cleavers well-heeled matrons who stay home because they *can*. The ranks of stay-at-home moms are swelling with women of all kinds, from the truly affluent to the newly poor (or *le nouveau pauvre*, as one of my former employees calls herself).

Though no one would promote poverty as a constructive solution to the work/family crunch, a growing number of people, men included, are finding that the kind of affluence they earn at work often comes with a steep price — not only for their children, but for themselves. And they're making a choice to forgo such affluence: to reduce debt, live more modestly, do without new cars and fancy clothes and upscale restaurants, and perhaps even retire those early retirement dreams in favour of living simply on a reduced household income so that one or both parents can afford to spend more time with the kids.

Of course, downshifting assumes certain financial resources to begin with. Not everyone can do it — which brings up a delicate question: Just because not everyone can afford to spend more time at home, does this diminish the value of my decision to do so? This is indeed how it feels, for women who "retreat" from work. And this is why at-home moms tend to be so quiet. We are diminished by having done "the wrong thing" in a society that empowers paid workers. We have quit the pack, renouncing the rule book that unites modern working women. A pay cheque is power? Not in our books it isn't. Financial independence? We can live without it, for a little while (though we understand that to do so is risky, and to do so long term is downright foolish). If we are comfortable with the personal risks and compromises of staying home — not for life, but for the period of time it takes to do some essential, unpaid work there — why should we feel judged? Of course we shouldn't, but we do, because for thirty years the *working woman* has set the standard for all women in our society. She is held up as the model against whom all others are measured; she has created the benchmarks for sexual equality and self-sufficiency. Measured against her, the stay-at-home mom is destined to come up short.

The pro-work bias is so strong in our society that it's easy to lose sight of the great number of women who don't work outside the home. We often hear that the dual-income family is now the norm, but in fact there's a parent at home in nearly half of all two-parent families with children under six, according to both Statistics Canada and the US Census Bureau. Though the majority of married women with school-age children do hold jobs, only about one-third of them work full-time, year-round. Among those who have full-time-working husbands, that figure drops to about one-fifth.

Despite the well-publicized pressure on families to bring in two incomes, there has been no decline over the past few years in the number of married mothers who do not work full-time. And it appears that in many cases nothing (save their kids) is holding them back. Employed mothers are more than six times as likely as employed fathers to hold part-time jobs, according to the New York–based Families and Work Institute. In the contingent (or contract) sector, four-fifths of mothers who work part-time do so by choice. And there are plenty of others who do not work for money at all. When college-educated women are surveyed separately, as *Working Woman* magazine did in 1996, we find that close to half of these women, despite qualifications for well-paying jobs and despite a variety of childcare options, prefer to stay home full-time with their kids.

There are many ways of envisioning a "model" for success: Superwoman is one of them; June Cleaver is another. Most working moms fall somewhere in between. . . .

My neighbour, Mary Keast, who recently quit a senior banking job to have her third child, still has difficulty responding when someone asks her what she does. "The way they say it, it sounds more like 'Who are you?' than 'What do you do?'" says Mary, balancing little Anna on her hip. "I'm trying to get used to saying 'I'm a mom,' but I often find myself muttering something like 'for now' at the end of it, so they won't think I'm *just* a mom. Somehow we assume that's not enough."

Because so many women, like Mary, tend to slip quietly out of the labour force, then slip quietly back in later, the at-home interlude is generally considered just that: an interlude. But the interlude can last for many years, and during this time we have a chance to do great work. While some seem to have trouble articulating the value of this work, the statistics show just how highly many women do value it, and how willing we are to compromise our work "out there" in order to heed the calling "in here."

The stats I'm talking about are the ones that demonstrate how far women have *not* gotten, despite equal opportunities in many fields, despite the large numbers of young women who have been emerging from colleges and universities for the last three decades. Though this doesn't fit the stereotype of our liberated generation, it does match what most of us have observed at our workplaces: Statistically, the real strivers are young, unmarried, and childless. These are the women who are scoring more new jobs than men their age and earning as much as 95 per cent of what their male counterparts do. As children enter the equation, women lose their competitive edge and wages fall off sharply — a reflection of the deadly truth about interludes: that a leave of any kind is a compromise, and it's not what you want to do when you're plotting your all-important career arc. Hence, accolades to the superwoman who takes just a few days off to deliver a child into the world. "Good for her," say her male colleagues. "She's not missing a beat!" A few months can pose a real momentum problem when you're peaking in your career. A year or more out of the loop can cause irreparable damage — yet this is what millions of women *choose* to do, erecting their own glass ceilings and counting themselves privileged that they can.

The reason we ought to acknowledge these invisible women is not so that we can form another pack, or hold up a new role model for "all" women. That would be the flip side of the same tyrannical coin. The point is to recognize and celebrate the diversity of our needs, our desires, and our working/parenting styles. There are many ways of envisioning a "model" for success: Superwoman is one of them; June Cleaver is another. Most working moms fall somewhere in between, into the ranks of women who are slightly overworked, slightly underemployed, trying to make the best of a challenging situation.

This is the compromise zone, and it's where most of us working parents live. Though the majority of North American families do need two incomes to survive, relatively few need two full-time incomes, and (thank goodness) *very* few need two executive-level incomes. Though you can read the statistics as evidence of an overworked society, you can also read them as confirmation of strong counter-balancing traditions when it comes to families. Sexual prejudice and old-boy networks cannot begin to explain the numbers of women who compromise their career goals — who jump off the ladder, or refuse to climb up in the first place. Only *choice* can explain it.

THE VALUE OF OUR WORK

In my recent travels, I've come upon a number of stay-at-home women's groups who are fighting hard to be counted. And they call themselves feminists, though they're on the fringe and proud of it. On the Canadian front, a national organization called Mothers Are Women (MAW) has been working for more than a decade to give voice to those who do the unpaid work of caring for their children and families. The Ottawa-based organization provides an important support network for women at home through its quarterly journal, *Homebase*, and newsletter, *The Kitchen Table Revolution* (for contact information, see page 225). MAW also provides a political platform on which to campaign for "true" equality — which they see as a giant step beyond the standard feminist definition of the term.

In feminism's desire to free women from unpaid work, the movement has left all that valuable work out of the equation, says MAW spokeswoman Evelyn Drescher. "By accepting male norms and fighting for equality on male terms, they devalue women's experiences and skills." MAW believes that only when unpaid household work is given economic value will the women who do it gain social and political visibility. To that end, MAW formed a coalition with several other Canadian women's groups to lobby for a crucial change in the 1996 Census — to have the unpaid work of family and elder care, household management and maintenance, planning and budgeting all counted as "work" for the purpose of data measurement. The lobby was successful, and the results will be released in 1998 — a first not only for Canada, but for the world.

Why is this important? Because beyond its obvious social value, the unpaid work that is done primarily by women — and in most cases by women who do paid work on top of it — has tremendous economic value to our society. Indeed, the health and commerce of our society depends upon this work, as Shirley Burggraf points out in *The Feminine Economy and Economic Man*. Yet women who do this work are not considered to be economic contributors: The housewife is glorified at best, impoverished at worst. The product of our considerable labour is not included in the Gross National Product, nor is it considered in the formulation of economic policy. Until the 1996 Census, unpaid "women's work" was uncounted, unvalued, and invisible. At least now, thanks to MAW, it has been counted.

> **Unpaid work that is done primarily by women—and in most cases by women who do paid work on top of it—has tremendous economic value to our society.**

Unfortunately, there are no guarantees the data will be used to promote the equality of women, concedes Drescher, or even that it will be used at all. "It may only amount to symbolic recognition intended to pacify women, rather than to change how society views and organizes work." Which means that MAW and its sister organizations have their work cut out for them, translating raw data into the seeds of social change. Drescher tries to be realistic.

> While somewhere over the rainbow we might get paid for this work, it isn't my personal goal. It is not the unpaid nature I am concerned with, but the invisibility, discrimination, and exclusion that goes along with not working for pay. But the valuation is important, as anyone going into divorce court or trying to settle an accident claim as a 'homemaker' or trying to enter the paid workforce again knows.

Is it even possible to put a dollar value on homemaking? Statistics Canada, using estimates based on its General Social Surveys, has come up with two methods of valuation that give two different results — one low, one high. The low valuation says a woman who is at home caring for her own children (one of whom is under seven) is doing work worth about $17,000 a year. MAW regards this as an extreme undervaluation of women's work, based as it is on an income-replacement model that uses service-sector wages rather than professional fees. In other words, according to this model, a woman who shops for fresh food, prepares high-quality meals, and caters special family occasions is valued not as a chef, but as a short-order cook. Likewise, she is not a chauffeur but a taxi driver to her children, and not a mentor but a babysitter.

By these standards, the economic contribution of all the home-making work being done annually in Canada is $285 billion. Because Statistics Canada recognizes that this figure is too low, they also offer their high-value method, based not on replacement but on opportunity — in other words, calculated on the basis of what the woman might earn if she were to work for pay rather than stay home. This method is actually a nightmare of inequity, because it makes a doctor's or lawyer's unpaid contributions to the household far more valuable than the same contribution made by, say, a nurse or secretary. All the same, using this method, Statistics Canada comes up with an average annual homemaker's salary of $26,310 — or $318.8 billion nationally.

A third model of valuation uses pay-equity scales common to many private Canadian companies. It is based on skills, effort, responsibility, and working conditions, and focuses on the work itself rather than on who is doing it. In this model, management of a household budget rates management-level fees. Tutoring and intensive counselling work with children is calculated on teaching scales. The stay-at-home mom's kitchen duties are measured on a sliding scale, from bottle-washer to gourmet chef. For these duties, our hypothetical mom nets about $38,000 a year. (A similar system was used by the American group Hearts at Home, to arrive at an annual income of $36,348, which boils down to $8.32 an hour for the homemaker's typical twelve-hour day.)

"This is the valuation method with which to go, ladies," advises Evelyn Dreschler of MAW. After all, managing a household *is* just like managing a small business — if not tougher. Mentoring children *is* very similar to mentoring staff, though much more is at stake with your kids. By bringing work-equity scales into our homes, we train ourselves to acknowledge, daily, that our work is not only valuable but transferable. And we live in hope that one day soon the working world will agree — that when we write "homemaker" on our résumés to account for a two- or five- or fifteen-year pause between paid jobs, we will be credited for having done something useful and *valuable* with that time. Such a pause, in such a world, will no longer be professional suicide.

MEET MR. JUNE CLEAVER

If I told Shaw I had a $38,000-a-year job here at home, but that the cheque was in the mail, would he respect me more, or simply think me an idiot? Would he join my wishful thinking that some day an employer will look at my résumé and raise an impressed eyebrow at my many valuable household management skills, and usher me into the corner office? "Get a grip," is what Shaw is more likely to say. "And where's my other brown sock?"

I have to work at not slagging my husband for his lack of faith, because I know the last few years have been as hard on him as they've been on me. Maybe harder — or at least more surprising. Here he thought we were through the worst of the work/family crunch and were gaining on that still-distant goal of early retirement, when I announced that I wasn't going to keep working like a maniac any more and that he could retire himself right out of the marriage if he wasn't ready to support me in this. (I've been accused of pig-headedness, not to mention short-sightedness. Who, exactly, was going to support me if he left?) Fortunately, Shaw has stepped into the Chief Bread-winner role, like my dad did all those years while my mom stayed home, but for which Shaw reaps none of the kid-glove treatment my dad used to get from my mom.

Kid gloves are simply not in my wardrobe. I must have burned them with the bras — a legacy of my early feminist training. I expect Shaw to work full-time *and* to be my equal partner in raising the children and running the house. I expect him not only to shop for groceries on the weekend, but to give me a call on his way home from work to see if there's anything I need him to pick up, and not to bluster if I ask for tampons. I expect him to unload a full dishwasher, not just stare at it. I expect him to read to the kids for at least fifteen minutes before nodding off, to fix the plumbing, remember our anniversary, and give me back-rubs — not every night, but *some* nights, for which I will do the same and much more in return, with the exception of plumbing. Shaw is not sure about the fairness of all this, and calls my approach "convenience feminism," about which I laugh before giving him the next order. The result is that Shaw often feels he can't do anything right, and maybe that's true. After all, as Dolly Parton used to say, he's just a man.

Shaw is not the only husband and father in the throes of an expectation crisis. As a rash of surveys has demonstrated over the past few years, husbands across North America and most of Europe fall far short of their wives' equity guidelines. In Canada, women prepare 76 per cent of the meals in their homes, are responsible for childcare 71 per cent of the time, and do 59 per cent of the shopping and other housework — yet we cling (hopelessly? irrationally?) to the notion of fifty-fifty partnership. Will our incessant whining ever produce results? Should we simply give up the equity ghost? Over our dead bodies.

Marital squabbling over the division of household chores is endemic to modern life. Perhaps it has always been thus, but it's certainly getting worse with increased out-of-home workloads for both partners. This may explain the jarring results of a 1996 Royal Bank–Angus Reid poll which showed that, as a group, the happiest people in Canada are widows. No joke: 65 per cent of widows said they are very satisfied with life, compared to 61 per cent of married women, and 43 per cent of single women.

Not all husbands get the gears, from daylight to dark. I have learned from my stay-at-home moms' e-mail group (see Resources, page 232) that some husbands do handily meet labour-of-love quotas while managing to bring home the bacon. Of the 125 women on this list, about a dozen have husbands who qualify as "good" in this way. Allow me to take you on-line, with a sampling of posts generated by a recent discussion entitled "DH Trouble." (DH, as you'll see in the glossary below, stands for dear husband. SAHM stands for stay-at-home mom). For those of you with DH trouble of your own, this brief dispatch may serve as a useful catharsis. And for those who wonder what SAHMs actually do all day long — well, listen up.

But before we get to DH Trouble, I ought to describe the women on this list. Most call themselves feminists, while at the same time questioning what that means. Several work part-time, though few have to leave home to do so. Most are in their thirties, with very young children, and there are always at least three who are pregnant. Discussions (about everything and anything) are marked by a high level of mutual respect and ongoing gratitude for having found one another in cyberspace. One of my e-pals, Alex, captures the tone perfectly in this post, which came at the end of a debate over the merits of sweatpants, the hypocrisy of lipstick, and the etiquette of dressing up for company.

> First off, I support Jessica's right to abhor sweats, Lisa's right to wear lipstick and Althea's right to wear skirts. And I think we should be able to post our opinions here freely. This group has what, 100+ members? We're united in being mothers and feminists, but that's about all. We're in different states and countries; we're married, single, lesbian; Jewish, Christian, Pagan, freethinkers; aged 20–60; we have different races, backgrounds, economics — BUT THAT'S WHAT MAKES THIS GROUP SO GREAT!!! Only through this medium can so many women come together and talk about our lives. Even our uniting factors are different: some of us are mothering toddlers, others teenagers. I suspect our definitions of feminism vary widely too — but, THAT'S WHAT MAKES THIS GROUP SO GREAT!!

Now, on to DH Trouble. Enter at your own risk. Watch for flying emotions, razor-sharp insults, runaway capitalizations, and exclamation marks galore!! Though some names have been changed to protect privacy, all participants consented to publication of this discussion. If you need to brush up on your cyberspeak, start by skimming this glossary:

sahm	stay-at-home mom
wah	work at home (paid)
woh	work outside home
dh	dear (or whatever) husband
rl	real life, as opposed to cyber
lol	laugh out loud
:)	smile
;)	wink
imho	in my humble opinion
btw	by the way
posting	sending a message
lurking	reading, not posting

>Suzanne: How do we get beyond resentment, ladies. I'm feeling lately that we don't have much of a life together outside of John's work schedule, and so when he works half of the weekend and then spends the rest of the time resting up, or recovering from a cold, invariably I resent it. Am I just being mean and selfish, or is this a valid complaint? I need some perspective.

>Danielle: In my marriage, whenever I am not working for money, the power structure in our relationship is all out of whack. Just yesterday while I was doing the room-mother thing at a holiday party, dh, who was there to watch our two youngest children so that I could participate in the party,

said something to the effect of, "Is this party going to be over soon? I need to get back to work. I am providing the sole income, blah blah blah." With that one statement, I felt like I was unimportant, and dependent upon him. We earn just about the same income when we are both woh'ing. We have similar skills/positions. He, however, has had the benefit of more education, more opportunity and much less time out of the work path than I have had. Same family, same goals, same life (we started dating in highschool!) and he is providing the SOLE income! We have had this same disagreement three times in our lives — the three times that I have been home with kids. Each time I get more angry. When I am working I feel like I have control over more of my time. If I am sick or need some space of my own, I can take a vacation day and spend the day doing whatever I want. When I am home, I have to depend on him for time away from a job that never ends (as well you know). Now when I need some time, I have to barter with him; he is doing me a favor. The core of this is that we are equally qualified to be the income-providing partner or stay-at-home partner. We could switch positions and our lifestyle would change very little — except that I have the breasts and value the breastfeeding relationship that I have with our infant daughter (pumping is not cool for me). So once again, I find myself angry, resentful, exhausted and in need of a day away! But mostly, I am hurt and discouraged and I feel very far away from dh — we are out of whack again. I would really appreciate some of your opinions. Maybe I am not able to see the whole picture because of my strong feelings.

>Harriet: I usually do (or arrange) most of the household jobs. I'm the one here more, so it makes much more sense. I don't think we ever really thought about it. Maybe I have a fair model. Since my mom started working full-time when I was a teen, my dad always had a much more flexible sched-

ule, so he was the one to wait for the plumber, electrician, etc. It always seemed logical that the one for whom it is more convenient (or less inconvenient) take care of things, gender aside. Dh and I also tend to get "bugs up our asses" about projects, which are not necessarily shared. He wanted the cable TV run into the office and I didn't care, so HE got the supplies and crawled into the attic to do it. Last week I decided to organize our coat closet. I went to Home Depot and got the stuff and installed it all myself.

>Laurel: I guess I should be very happy and grateful because dh is really great around the house and with the kids — and yet, I still complain sometimes! (Especially in my current pregnant state.) Actually, when he's here, he probably does much more of the childcare than I do — he makes their dinners most nights, and usually handles toothbrush time. He also does the laundry, mops the floors, and shares the vacuuming (although I do the rest of it). And when I was in school full-time, this never made me feel guilty — but now that I'm home, I do feel guilty when he does so much. I feel like I'm damned if I do, damned if I don't: I either feel guilty that he helps so much, or I would feel mad if he didn't! And yet, I can't imagine him feeling guilty about what I do on the domestic front! In this sense, I agree with Danielle that the power structure goes out of whack when one partner stops earning money. I do notice that when I have stayed home full-time in the past without going to school or having a wah project, I feel that our relationship is more strained — I feel resentful about doing housework and other tasks that I HATE. When I'm working, I feel like my household work is contributing to the family rather than being solely my responsibility that he "helps" with. Rather upside-down logic, but there you go!

>Sheena: I had a fight with dh last night and I'm feeling pretty bad. He owns his own business, and works long and

stressful hours. When deadlines loom, invariably he gets sick. This is a real pattern in his life. He exercises regularly, goes to bed early and eats well so go figure? Anyway, I'm really not a sympathetic person when it comes to him being ill (and he's not exactly a good patient) and I find I get pretty annoyed with him because he wants me to mother him. I feel overwhelmed with my role as mother to my children at the best of times, and so I really react badly to him wanting to be coddled (btw, illness was not well tolerated in my family when I was growing up).

>Andrea: I know this feeling well! No sympathy here! Which is so weird because actually there are a lot of times when I do "just" want sympathy, and dh feels quite strident about giving me his VIEWS and his ADVICE and not just a little tea (a caress?) & sympathy! My husband too has an almost sublime ability to get sick when big deadlines at work come off. And it seems I'm always paying the price — I get him through the week by taking the load, then expect him to chip in on the weekend, only to find him needing bed rest and quiet come weekend. Poor baby!

>Harriet, later the same day: Money=power was an issue when I first became sah. I think it was much more an issue for me than for dh. He never really thought much about it and didn't bring it up, except in a rare fight. We started sharing money as soon as we became engaged, even before we were living together. Both our parents always shared money, so there was really no question. We never even discussed it, we just did it. We did recently discuss both our feelings on my sah status. Dh is quite happy with it as long as I am. He said that my being home enables him to do his job the way he does (usually 12-plus-hour days) so that benefits the whole family. He did not mean it in a chauvinistic way. He KNOWS that I work hard. He wouldn't want to trade places. (I also think part

of it is a male ego thing about being able to "support his family in a comfortable lifestyle.") If/when I want to go back to work/school, that will be fine with him and he will do what he has to do (I think). But he likes knowing that the kids are well cared for and the house is run, etc. I do think that it would be difficult for him to cut down on his hours significantly (it's the way he is and always has been), so I'll always be the one "running" things around the house. I really don't mind. I kind of like being the one "in charge" and in control of our home. Sometimes it feels strange when he is home early in the evening. My "regular" routine doesn't involve him. I guess that if I ever decide to do something else on more than a part-time basis, we'll have to negotiate and adjust.

EX-FILE | *Teacher Overboard*

NAME: Suzanne Whitely, 36

EX: Elementary school teacher

CURRENT: Stay-at-home mom

RÉSUMÉ HIGHLIGHTS: BS in education; MA in curriculum development; taught primary grades in Chicago's public school system, 1984–95.

PERSONAL: Married; one daughter, Grace, 1.

BACKGROUND: Ever since I was a young child I knew I wanted to be two things — a mommy and an elementary school teacher. I was lucky during college to already be sure what I wanted to study, then to love it once I finished my preparation for the field. It was intellectually challenging to develop curriculum appropriate to that specific group of students, and I relished the opportunity to spend my life doing something I loved so much. My friends, by and large, were my colleagues, so I loved going to work for both professional and personal reasons. Talk about fulfilment — except for one thing: I still wanted a child.

I became pregnant in my eleventh year of teaching. As a high-risk patient (I have a seizure disorder), the pregnancy was difficult at times, and my friends at school were a wonderful support system. My last day I cried all the way home. I knew having a baby was what I wanted, but it was so difficult leaving my friends and career. The district policy offered generous parental leave, plus a guaranteed job on return — though not necessarily in the same school or grade level. When I left that day, I was fairly sure I would not be with my friends again. It was the end of a very fulfilling, challenging part of my life.

REDEFINITION: After Grace was born, I had a tough adjustment. So much of my identity revolved around teaching — I suddenly had to redefine myself in terms of life without students. Though we'd lived in our house three years by then, I knew few neighbours who were home during the day. Without a social support system, that first year was very hard.

I planned to apply for a team-teaching position on my return. I wanted to work half-time, which would create some financial hardship but would at least serve to save my space in the district until I was ready to go back full-time. I had to start the application procedure when Grace was eleven months old. A full-time mother once told me it took about twelve months before things fell into place after the birth of a child. I was a little slower; at thirteen months it hit me that I was no longer sure I wanted to go back to teaching, even part-time. But if I didn't go back now, I might be jeopardizing my professional future. So I made the application.

THE CHALLENGE: I was given my assignment in April of '95 — I'd be placed in a kindergarten class at a new school. Soon I began going to meetings in preparation for the new year. My vast experience with kindergarten involved a semester of teaching five children, mornings only, thirteen years ago. After six years of third grade, I knew I had some learning to do. By fall, I thought I was prepared — professionally, at least.

First days are often tough, but my first one in that kindergarten class was beyond my worst nightmare. I was still learning the curriculum and completely unprepared for the drastic difference between kindergarten students and the others I'd taught. These are babies. They're often leaving parents for the first time, and are just learning the social skills necessary for the rest of their school career. I thought I was prepared for my Downs syndrome student, but realized immediately that I really didn't know what I could expect from him behaviourally or academically — how hard should I push? I also had three children who didn't speak English, one of whom had severe behavioural problems. How much attention should I take from other students to help these three with their special needs?

For the first few weeks, I was spending ten to twelve hours a day, six days a week, trying to organize and plan so our days would live up to my expectations. In the second month, things started falling into place, and I was only spending six to eight hours a day for my half-time job. I was starting to think this situation was workable, if just barely.

THE TURNING POINT: I felt I was coping most days, but when something out of the ordinary happened at school, everything fell apart. For example, I always used to welcome an opportunity to meet with parents, and assumed I could handle whatever concerns came up. But now, when parents contacted me, I would worry for days (and nights) before the meeting. Or when Grace got sick at day care, I felt horrible for not being there to care for her. When a meeting was scheduled beyond day-care hours, I found myself angry that my personal time was being infringed upon. Even if the meeting was of great interest, I had to talk myself into taking a positive attitude so I'd be able to get something out of it. I didn't like what I felt developing. I was starting to think I couldn't be a good mother and a good teacher at the same time.

Then my health declined. After fighting a chronic illness for fifteen years, I had finally gotten it under control during my maternity leave. Three weeks into the school year, it returned and I realized my body was telling me what my heart already knew: This was too much. It was too much time, energy, and stress. I needed to be raising my daughter, not educating others' children right now. The best of me was going to work; my family was getting the leftovers.

Being exhausted, short of patience, and frustrated at the end of a day was bad enough. Being sick and trying to recover with whatever remaining energy I had was just too much. My doctor, concerned about the severity of my seizures, wrote a letter to the school district and they agreed to grant a health leave.

I am still on leave, but have decided to resign when it expires. There are times I regret having started back at something that I couldn't sustain — but then I remind myself that I couldn't have known whether this would work out until I tried it. I know it does work well for many; it just wasn't right for me. We can only make decisions with available information.

Right now, I'm trying not to plan anything professionally. Maybe I'll do some tutoring for now; one day I might get involved in college instruction of student teachers, or get back into curriculum development. What I know is that I want to create a nurturing, exciting, rich environment in which Grace can develop. When she no longer needs so much of my time, I'll consider the next step in my career.

TAKE-OUT WISDOM: Grace will probably be our only child, and the thought of never experiencing all the "firsts" I can made me realize how precious this time is. Once my health declined, I was reminded how much we take for granted. Who knows if I'll be able to get my health under control again?

When I'm having trouble, I'm unable to do anything. If I permanently lost the ability to do all the things that are important to me, I would forever regret the time spent doing "what I was supposed to do." Thinking "there'll always be next year to enjoy time with my family" was just not good enough for me.

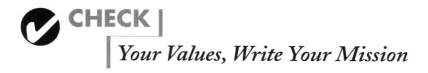

CHECK |
Your Values, Write Your Mission

1. HOW TO SORT YOUR VALUES

This exercise comes from Stacey Mayo, a vocational counsellor whose Atlanta-based Center for Balanced Living specializes in helping people find work that best suits their skills and passions. Among her assessment tools is Inherit Values™, which is a way of identifying the values at play in our lives — those we've inherited from parents, employers, mentors, and society in general. Identifying and sorting values is by no means the fast track to your next job, but it can get you pointed in the right direction by allowing you to embrace your core values and discard the ones that are holding you back. Stacey employs a number of visualization and clarification exercises in combination with her Inherit Values program to make it effective. As with most vocational therapy, a full diagnostic session can take a week or more. What's given here will just give you a taste.

"Often these values run our lives at a subconscious level," says Stacey. "Many of us move through life as if through a tunnel, going straight forward, dealing with whatever comes our way, and then moving forward again. These *inherited values* are always in the background, affecting our decisions as we move from point A to point B to point C.

"My own mom valued safety and perseverance, and that

pretty much ruled the decisions made in our household. Dad valued beauty and perfectionism. My parents' generation valued hard work as the way to survive. My culture, Judaism, values intelligence and achievement. When I was growing up, society placed high value on the traditional family, much as it does today: husband and wife, two kids, a house, and a dog — until death do us part.

"I followed my inherited values for many years. I lived a pretty stable life: was smart and achievement-oriented, climbed my way up the corporate ladder, and reached a high level of recognition and monetary success. I got married at age 23, built a nice house with plenty of beautiful furnishings, owned a boat, etc.

"Over the years, as I got in touch with what did and didn't work for me, I moved on. I left an unhappy marriage at age 32, and my 'successful' career at 38. I was the first in my family to do either. In each case, I found that my ladder was leaning up against the wrong wall. Being married for the sake of being married was not enough for me, and my career, although quite an achievement, no longer seemed to fit. In looking back, I can now see that the biggest thrill my promotion to Vice President brought was receiving flowers from my parents, not from the title.

"We often live out our parents' desires and expectations for us rather than our own. I see it time and time again with my clients — creative dreams squashed because someone said, You can't make a living doing *that*, or they watched their parents suppress their own dreams and modelled their own behaviour after them. I had a client who showed me two pictures hanging on his walls. One was of his mom as a flamenco dancer and the other was a watercolour his dad had painted. He said to me, "Both my parents were artists, but they lived as accountants." He, too, was living in his parents' footsteps and suppressing his own creative talents.

"What are the values you inherited? How many of those still fit for you?"

Values Clarification Exercises

In clarifying your values, use the list of "Sample Values" as a guideline, and add any others that may apply. Note two basic types of values: those you aspire to, and those you use to bring your aspirations to life. Start by identifying the values you've inherited from your parents, your culture, and your mentor/boss. If these categories don't fit your life, customize them: guardians instead of parents, geographic environment instead of culture, teacher/minister instead of boss/mentor, etc. You may have to guess at values you're not sure of, especially in the mentor category. Base your guess on the way they live their lives and the things they've said or done that impressed you. After filling out the four categories, circle those values you believe have shaped your life by influencing your decision making. Then cross out those that have influenced what you would consider poor decisions.

Inherited Values

MOM'S VALUES	DAD'S VALUES
1.	1.
2.	2.
3.	3.
4.	4.
5.	5.

MY CULTURAL VALUES	MENTOR/BOSS'S VALUES
1.	1.
2.	2.
3.	3.
4.	4.
5.	5.

Sample Values

ASPIRED VALUES	FUNCTIONAL VALUES
(what you aspire to have)	(how you attain aspired values)
☐ Achievement	☐ Accountability/ Responsibility
☐ Adventure	
☐ Balance	☐ Affection
☐ Beauty	☐ Autonomy
☐ Community	☐ Communication
☐ Contribution	☐ Competency
☐ Family	☐ Courtesy
☐ Freedom	☐ Courage
☐ Friendship	☐ Creativity
☐ Fun	☐ Discipline
☐ Health	☐ Drive
☐ Justice	☐ Fairness
☐ Love	☐ Flexibility
☐ Nature/Environment	☐ Forgiveness
☐ Partnership	☐ Giving
☐ Peace	☐ Honesty
☐ Power	☐ Humor
☐ Recognition	☐ Knowledge
☐ Self-Worth	☐ Loyalty
☐ Spirituality	☐ Organization
☐ Stability	☐ Reason
☐ Wealth	☐ Safety
☐ Wisdom	☐ Team
	☐ Tolerance

2. HOW TO WRITE A MISSION STATEMENT

Taking an inventory of your values is one step towards clarifying what's essential to you. But how can you use that knowledge to redefine your work and rebalance your life? That's a tough question, but you're wise to address it if you want to make a successful transition in your work. Career counsellors are near unanimous in embracing this challenge, making it the modern equivalent of the old "vocational test." Instead of taking stock of your skills (word processing, drill press operating) you take stock of your competencies, natural strengths, values, and desires.

One tool in the new counselling kit is the personal mission statement. This is an adaptation of a traditional focusing/motivating technique used by organizations looking to clarify their goals in order to achieve positive change. It's more of a trial-and-error tool than an exact science, and can't be done quickly. Indeed, a personal mission statement can take a lifetime to create because we are never done changing, seeking, and clarifying.

Use what you've learned about your core values to draft your mission statement. It can be written as a promise to yourself ("In everything I do, I will….") or as a fond description of you at your best ("In everything I do, I endeavour to….") The intent of a mission falls somewhere between *who you are* and *who you'd like to be*, which means you can write it in the present or future tense. For me, the present carries more power and averts wishful thinking. It also forces me to take into account the values I have more than the ones I would like to have, recognizing that after a certain age my values are not likely to change all that much. But there's plenty of room for change in what I do with those values.

Although this is a departure from tradition, you may want to include past accomplishments in your mission. The more detail you are able to include — on past jobs, volunteering, hobbies, and even childhood achievements — the more you will learn from the exercise. Acknowledge weaknesses, but don't waste time hunting for them. This is supposed to be about your strengths.

If you draw a blank within moments of starting your mission statement, don't be alarmed. You have to warm to this task. One way to focus your thoughts is to share them with someone close to you. Your best friend may have some stunningly accurate observations about your nature that you'd never have guessed at if you hadn't asked. Use this as a tool to open what might be one of the best dialogues you've had in years. (You can help your friend with her/his mission at the same time.) In fact, this exercise can be done within a small group of friends, as a kind of social job-search exercise. Ask your friends what kind of work they think you'd be good at, and why. The "why" is critical, because it allows them to dig up fond memories of you at your best. Within a supportive atmosphere, this can be both constructive and fun. But a word of caution: Use your friends' input to expand on your own thoughts, not to replace them.

Set up your mission statement in any way that works best for you: in a diary or scrapbook or even on loose sheets kept in a box. Add art, poetry, inspirational quotes, and any other elements that enhance the transformational power of the exercise. This ought to be a labour of love, so the best time to approach it is when your mind is free to wander; the best place is where you are most comfortable and private. Light a candle, put on some favourite music, soak in a bath to prime yourself, then enjoy. When you run out of ideas or enthusiasm, put it aside for another day. Once you've begun, you'll find yourself storing away mental notes and looking forward to your next mission moment. Here's an outline to get you started:

- In everything that I do, I endeavour to _____.
- My deepest beliefs are _____.
- My destiny is _____.
- I am uniquely able to _____.

- What my family needs me to do is _____.
- What my community/neighbourhood/church/city needs me to do is _____.
- I have most fun when I _____.
- My strongest attributes are _____.
- Those who know me best say I am _____.
- I consider myself blessed if every single day I am able to _____.
- My greatest satisfaction derives from _____.
- I am proudest of myself when _____.
- I do my best work when _____.
- What I would most like to change in my life is _____.
- This change enriches my life by _____.
- I can find help and support from/by _____.
- My first step towards change is _____.
- My reward for accomplishing this is _____.

Include: my inventory of past jobs/tasks/accomplishments: What have I done? What have I done particularly well? What patterns emerge? What explanations can I find?

FIVE

The Long Human Childhood

THAT WAS THEN	THIS IS NOW
Parental leave	Parental life
Faking time	Making time
Quality	Quantity
Training	Modelling
Managing	Nurturing
Convenience	Passion
Planning	Living
Guilt	Pride
Work first	Children first

When a child arrives, your life changes — profoundly, and for good. All of us experience this, if not all to the same degree. Though warnings are broadcast by those who've fallen into the family way before us, it is impossible to be truly prepared for the stunning overnight changes a child brings to a marriage, to friendships, pastimes, finances, even politics. Our lives are turned upside down in every way — except at work, where we pretend it's business as usual. Oh, we may take some time off — a few months, or even a few years. But the minute we return to our jobs it's as though we'd never been away. The in-tray is just a little fuller, and the boss a little hungrier for results. This is the charade that creates virtually single workers — men and women whose outward appearance suggests a single-minded focus on work that belies how profoundly distracted they are by their children and by the work of being parents.

This unnatural situation at work can engender an unnatural situation at home, where stressed and guilty parents often do one of two things: Either they give their kids extremely wide latitude, or no latitude at all. The wide-latitude kids, regularly placated by parents who feel they must compensate for all the time they spend away from the nest, learn early how to wangle and whine for what they want. They become adept at manipulating, stalling, negotiating. They become, in short, omnipotent. The no-latitude kids, the ones who are not allowed to rock the boat at home because their parents' stress-fractured nerves can't take it, generally get their revenge later. They become omnipotent at adolescence, when they're capable of rocking much more than the boat. What goes around comes around, as they say.

Of course this is a generalization, but I've seen similar scenarios played out again and again in many families, including my own. My kids fell through more than a few cracks in the years when both Shaw and I were working full-time at high-stress jobs. They couldn't help but be affected by a mother who modelled speed more than happiness, who ran the house like a military operation because any variation from routine could tip the delicate balance and derail the bullet train. I'd like to think this did no long-term damage, that my kids (like kids) are resilient and, as long as they are loved and taught some fundamental lessons in life, can survive much worse things than living with busy parents. But only time will tell.

TIME-DEFICIT PARENTING

Indeed, *time* is what it's all about. When you don't have much time with your children, you respond to them very differently than if you have a lot. You try to squeeze as much "positive parenting" as possible into every minute, trying to create the semblance of quality in the absence of quantity. From the outside, this can appear to be a lovely compromise — which is how some of my stay-at-home friends saw my life, back in the days when our kids were small and demanding. While I had the benefit of breezing in and out of my children's lives on my way to or from work, my friends were stuck at home for days, weeks, months on end, scraping peanut butter off cabinet doors, tweezing splinters out of baby toes, and endlessly refereeing siblings whose sole purpose in life was to bring their mother to tears. I had a nanny to do all this dirty work. When I arrived home, it was all fun and games. Or so thought my stay-at-home friends.

The truth is that, when I got home, it was mostly organization, negotiation, and compromise. There was far too much talk and far too little action — action like going out for a bike ride, mucking about with finger paints, or splashing in a bubble bath until the water is cold and there's more on the floor than in the tub. Most evenings, I didn't have the patience to take the bubble-bath test. Sometimes I could muster the mental energy for Lego, though large and complicated buildings were out of the question. "Build something with me, Mommy," someone would plead. "Not now, honey. Maybe after dinner." "Oh, please, Mommy — just one castle." "No. Not a castle. Okay, maybe a small castle. But give me ten minutes." "No, Mommy. Now!" "Five minutes." "Now!" "Okay, now...." At which point I would force myself onto my belly on the carpet and go through the motions of caring about the wretched castle, of actually enjoying its construction or taking pride in its hasty completion. The kids must have known I was faking it. The first clue was the speed with which I snapped those little blocks together. The second was the grimace that greeted my little architect's executive decision to tear it apart and try again. The third was the tumbler of wine beside me — right next to the cell phone. Within minutes, the charade would be over and the kids would be planted in front of a video so Shaw and I could catch our breath over dinner and synchronize our schedules for the next day.

Yes, we had time-deficit parenting down to an art form. We

succeeded in keeping the kids sufficiently happy and distracted to see us through those few hectic hours in the evening till they fell into bed and we could get back to the serious business of running our lives, and theirs. This approach cost us spontaneity, it cost us fun, it certainly cost us sincerity, but, most important, it cost us the opportunity to be mean — to say no to our kids when they needled us, to set limits when we saw them inching towards omnipotence, to lay out consequences for both good and bad behaviour, and to be there to follow through. Like a lot of working parents, we fell into the reward-and-distract trap. Just having us home felt like a reward to them, and we reinforced that impression by being as nice to them as possible. When they needed more from us, we found ways to distract them. We felt we were doing our best, given the shortage of time.

> **We had time-deficit parenting down to an art form. This approach cost us spontaneity, it cost us fun, it certainly cost us sincerity . . .**

Liza Wasser, an at-home mom I correspond with, captured the nub of the scheduling problem in a recent post from Germany, where she lives with her husband and five kids. Liza, by the way, is considered Queen Mom of the e-mail group you met in Chapter Four, and her husband Dave (a computer analyst who knits for fun) is King Dad. "Happy chaos" is how they describe their household. "One of the reasons I stay home with the kids is because I think they need more attention and care than even the best day-care situation can give," wrote Liza.

And because I don't need to work for money, I am able to choose this. I have also found that pushing and external schedules really mess up my mothering. I find that I am always short-tempered if I have to do anything with kids on any kind of schedule. Kids and timetables don't mix. So, I try to make as many things as possible be as flexible as they can. I only push when necessary. I will not take any nonsense if I have a train to catch. But if it's a non-train-catching day I will sing the "Mr. Plaque Teethbrushing Song" (by David Wasser, copyright 1981) so Alex will brush his teeth willingly and happily. I will play all kinds of silly dressing games if I have the time. I try to arrange my life so that there aren't too many train-catching days.

This is why I don't work outside my home. I don't wish to force small children into that kind of hectic schedule. And so, likewise, I don't force developmental issues. They weaned when they were ready. They ate solid food when they were ready. They slept through when they were ready. They toilet-trained when they were ready. I never gave myself ulcers weaning, training or teaching them to sleep through. I never even spoon-fed them. They were ready for solids when they could pick them up and put them in their own mouths. I figured it wasn't my job. It was theirs. Kids are smart. They can figure this stuff out all by themselves. You just have to give them time and space.

By comparison, when our children were small, they lived very much in our time and space. This was not only their loss, but ours — Shaw's and mine. We spent far too much of their early childhood scheduling for tomorrow when we all could have benefited from living for today, which is something the kids might have taught us if we'd made the time to learn. Stephan Rechtschaffen, author of the 1996 book *Time Shifting*, describes what can be gained when parents adjust to the natural pace of a child. Here's a time-shifting experience he shared with his youngest son, Eli, then three years old:

Lying together on a bed early one morning, we heard a bird. Its call was four beats, then a twenty-second pause, then another four beats, and so on: a steady, curiously cheerful rhythm that captivated Eli. We began to play a game, trying with a motion of a hand to note when the first beat would begin again. For five to ten minutes we entrained with the bird, lost in its rhythm. I could sense the expanding of the moment, a slowing down that resulted from our mindful attention. I was thrilled to see how my young child could stay so concentrated and present*

Young children have no sense of time, says Rechtschaffen. "They, like animals (which never learn time), can locate themselves in space from infancy, but the words 'later,' or 'soon,' or concepts like 'tomorrow' or 'next year' are meaningless even to a four-year-old. Past, present, and future are unknown to small children. They live in the moment — and we try to yank them out of it as soon as we can."

THE RECKONING

It is not only working parents who are guilty of hurrying their children. You might say our whole culture is inimical to the healthy development of kids. As a rule, we prefer to "manage" children rather than nurture them — both as a concession to our very busy lives and as a strategy to see them launched into busy, successful lives of their own. And it's never too early to start managing, as far as Type-A parents are concerned. Working and stay-at-home moms alike fall into the flashcard trap, imposing their own academic expectations and timetables on children who can barely say *cat*, never mind spell it. Even worse, children are placed in front of TVs to jump-start their schooling, as though the mind-jamming, Nintendo-paced editing techniques of shows such as *Sesame Street* are good for them. It is obvious to parents who are watching carefully that the main lesson kids carry away from those so-called educational shows is that sensory-overload learning is a lot more fun than the kind of learning unhurried children might be doing at the library. Or just at home, on the kitchen floor, with a playmate and a set of nesting cups. So why are we sur-

---

*Reprinted from *Time Shifting: Creating More Time to Enjoy Your Life*, Stephen Rechtscheffen, M.D., by permission of Doubleday, a division of Bantam Doubleday Dell Publishing Group, Inc.

prised when psychologists tell us we're raising a generation of attention-deficit kids? Did we think our sons and daughters would learn to stretch their attention spans in front of a TV or video monitor?

And why are we surprised when teachers complain that students don't know the meaning of civility, of common decency, of empathy? Did we think our kids would learn how to be humane by watching *Beverly Hills 90210*? Here is the most frightening consequence of our time crunch, the fallout of half-hearted child-rearing: We seem to be raising half-hearted children. It's easy to give our kids a leg up academically — even the busiest parent can find a few minutes in a day to run a math drill, and with the help of *Sesame Street* they'll be singing the alphabet by age three. It's much, much harder to impart a code of conduct based on a moral universe that is actually discussed around the dinner table, and that forms the basis of your family library. That's right, I said *library* — if not of books, then at least of videos, or CDs, or whatever it takes to create openings for talking, thinking, and growing. All of which takes far more time than most families have to spare.

A reckoning is in store, where kids are concerned. Indeed, if you've talked to a school counsellor lately, you'll know the reckoning is under way. While we've been busy taking the fast lane to success, a lot of our kids have been taking the fast lane somewhere else. Recent studies undertaken by the Carnegie Council on Adolescent Development indicate that about one-third of American teenagers have contemplated suicide, and half are at moderate to high risk of abusing drugs, failing in school, getting pregnant, or otherwise seriously damaging their lives. Although the risks are exacerbated by poverty, the Carnegie Council reported that "in survey after survey, young adolescents from all ethnic and economic backgrounds lament their lack of parental attention and guidance."

Canadian studies show the same kinds of trouble brewing across geographic and economic borders. Youth crime is up, with violent crime having more than doubled between 1986 and 1994, according to a new study by Simon Fraser University criminologists. Drug use among adolescents is at an all-time high and continuing to climb, according to Health Canada, and teenage pregnancy is rising too, which is not surprising considering that teenagers in the 1990s are having more sex, and having it an earlier age than we did. And they're likely to be having it at home, in the afternoon, in the empty houses of their working parents. "It's better than cars," reported a seventeen-year-old Toronto boy interviewed by *The Globe and Mail.* "There's less chance you'll be rushed."

A code of conduct is not something that can be taught during "quality time." Nor is education something that just *happens*, during school hours. Guiding our children towards positive outcomes is a daunting responsibility for time-pressed parents, but the consequences of failing to do so are much more daunting. The US Census Bureau reported in 1994 that the difference in lifetime earnings between a student who did not graduate from high school and one who did is more than $200,000. A student who received a university degree will make almost $1 million more than one who did not graduate from high school. And what is the single most important thing we can do to help our kids be successful in school? Read to them for an hour each night, say researchers at the US Department of Education. We all know we should be doing this, but who has the time, or the energy? According to surveys, only half of American parents with children under nine read to them daily.

American writer Nora Ephron might have been kidding when she said we should raise our children well, so they can pay for their own therapy — but there's a bit of truth in this. Raising them well is hard work, and it lasts many years. In her 1994 book *Children First,* Penelope Leach speaks of the "long human childhood."

We know much more about the reproductive biology and genetics of parenthood than we know about the social, emotional and psychological impacts of parenting and we devote far greater research resources to producing physically healthy babies than to rearing emotionally stable children. Indeed, while family planning, artificial baby foods and a host of childcare aids have dramatically reduced the burdens of traditional mothering roles, those roles themselves have been invalidated and have not been replaced with a workable restructuring of gender roles and relationships.[*]

Parental leave allows us to bond with our infants, but as soon as that's over, the rationing of time and attention begins, says Leach.

> The ending of infancy alters the necessary commitment of parents or their surrogates but does not end it. Children under seven still need constant adult protection. In middle childhood, survival and life skills, along with morals and manners, go on being learned over at least five more years of close apprenticeship to adults. Even then, on the edge of puberty, it takes people at least five further years of physical growth and intellectual and social maturation to refine those skills so that adolescents can begin to function as adults within the value system of their particular culture. However much they may delegate to other caregivers and to educational institutions, parents and parent figures are crucial to every phase of this long human childhood, not least because it is individual parents who most passionately want to meet the needs of their own children, and passion is part of what is needed.

Most of us do care passionately about bringing our kids up right, but we don't always do what is required to get this job done. We need, first of all, to acknowledge that children cannot run on adult schedules, or at least they *should* not. Children develop slowly, learn slowly (despite our best efforts to rush them), and require painstaking consistency from those who would help them to develop and learn well. "Be consistent" is the most popular piece of advice novice parents are given, and there is no denying its validity. A child who is expected to behave in a certain way, but who is allowed to behave in another, depending on his parents' moods and timetables, will learn a highly conditional lesson about behaviour. But how can we be consistent when we're not with that child for a large part of the day? Is it fair

[*]From *Children First*, by Penelope Leach, © 1994 by Penelope Leach; reprinted by permission of Alfred A. Knopf, Inc.

to discipline bad behaviour when the lesson was poorly taught? And how can we introduce discipline into those few "quality" moments we spend with our children, without ruining the quality, making the child angry and ourselves guiltier than ever?

There are good answers to all these questions, and many working parents have found them. But not without steadfast effort and organization. For example, if I am not going to be with my child for large parts of each day, it is my responsibility to ensure that the key lessons and values that I wish to impart to that child are understood by the caregiver, and that the caregiver has the means to impart them for me. Achieving consistency in this way can be very tricky. If my child goes to a day-care centre, it had better be a centre where the values and practices harmonize with the ones in our home. If my child is allowed to yell at another child at day care, in the interest of "using words instead of fists," then I need to know about such a strategy so I can reinforce it with consistency at home. Likewise, when a babysitter or nanny is employed, childcare methods and expectations must be discussed and clear ground rules laid. It is not enough for the child to survive until I finish my shift at work, nor is it useful to merely keep her entertained or distracted.

The same reasoning applies to older children, though managing their care is often more complicated. The work/family crunch can be devastating when inflexible schedules collide, but working parents of adolescents who understand the challenge, and who are committed to putting their children first, can usually find ways to adapt and thrive. Part-time, flex time, compressed work weeks, and telecommuting can significantly alleviate the work/family crunch, if not eliminate it entirely. If such options are not available at your workplace, group pressure might help to bring them about. If pressure doesn't work, a change of employer might be necessary. Something usually has to give when it comes to kids, and as a society, we've given too much to our employers lately. It's time to turn the tables, acknowledging this basic truth about parenting: that every moment of every day, my child is learning what life means as a member of this family and this society.

It seems so obvious, but still bears saying — as Dr. Benjamin Spock recently did in the tenth-anniversary edition of *Parenting* magazine, in May of 1997.

> The real problem is that many mothers and fathers take their work more seriously than they do their families. I believe we have to decide that family comes first and to make it clear to our children that they're more important than anything else in our lives. Even friendships, neighborhood activities, and cultural interests should take higher priority than jobs, because these are what humanize us and show our children what matters most. I don't want to get into an argument about whether or not Einstein's work should have been his first priority, but I am suggesting that during the childrearing years, parents shift their career into the background and bring the family into the foreground. This may be easy for me to say, but I think parents should make whatever sacrifices are necessary for that to happen — whether it means getting by on less income for several years or temporarily postponing certain goals and pursuits.*

Dr. Spock advocates subsidies, from government and/or employers, to compensate parents for making these financial sacrifices. He also urges an overhaul of the childcare system, with the state leading the way, in order to improve life for families in need of support. It is not only up to families to put children first, he argues. It is also up to the state, because we are raising the next generation together.

UPS AND DOWNS OF STAYING HOME

Many of us do believe our best option is to stay home, at least a good part of the time, and we struggle to find a way to do it. Often, our resolve in

*Reprinted by permission of *Parenting* magazine ©1997.

this matter takes us, as well as our partners and employers, very much by surprise. At close range, and with an infant in our arms, childcare options suddenly look quite different from what we'd envisioned. This is why managers who've been through a few turnovers of employees always shudder when a valuable staff member starts her maternity leave. Despite what she may say — and even what she may think — there's a good chance she'll decide not to return to full-time work.

One morning, on a break from my research, I opened my local newspaper and found a column under the "Voices" heading, written by a twenty-seven-year-old homemaker named Jennifer Genereux. Jennifer described how she had put her teaching career on hold in order to stay home and look after her son, Dallas. To ease the financial pressure on her husband, Jennifer looked into becoming a day-care provider, taking one or two neighbourhood children into her home on weekdays. After taking training and passing the rigorous requirements of a licensing agency, she broached the subject of pay. The agency rep informed her that she could charge $24 for the full-day care of one child.

I was in shock. Surely parents don't expect someone to do the important job of raising their child for $24 a day? When I asked how people could do it for so little pay, I was told most caregivers take in three or four children in addition to their own. But I wanted to provide a loving, attentive and educational environment; not a diaper, food and activity assembly line. I know I couldn't give each child the care he or she deserves with such a high ratio — who could? I turned down the job.

> Most stay-at-home moms know, however, that the line between blessing and curse can be a fine one. A full-scale retreat from the work world can spell a dangerous brand of dependence . . .

Jennifer Genereux is not June Cleaver. Nor is she one of Faith Popcorn's "have-it-all" moms of the 1990s. Materially, she has moderate needs.

But like many young women of her generation, Jennifer has a clear sense of her own values. "Too often, parents expect the life of their child to be nurtured and safeguarded for less than the parent makes before coffee break," she says. "Sadly, in a society fond of bragging about the priority it places on children, the reality is that most people value themselves over their children."

While this rings true to many of us, the implications are far from clear. Should we start ironing the diapers, as feminist columnist Barbara Ehrenreich puts it? "No culture on earth outside of mid-century suburban America has ever deployed one woman per child without simultaneously assigning her such major productive activities as weaving, farming, gathering, temple maintenance, and tent-building," wrote Ehrenreich in her 1989 book *The Worst Years of Our Lives.* "The reason is that full-time, one-on-one child-raising is not good for women or children." Is this a broadside, or a fact? What harm does staying home, long term, do to us? And what does it teach our children? That we've been put on this earth to create and nurture a new life, at the expense of our own? Perhaps sacrifice of this kind is, indeed, the natural and necessary state of early motherhood, but how long can it be sustained, and at what price? And why should women be making that sacrifice, and not men?

Virtually all the at-home moms I've spoken with confess to struggling with such questions, and to having days when they feel a distinct lack of reward for their costly choice. Doing some kind of volunteer or paid work from home provides some relief, but for many women this remains scant compensation for having left a career in midstream. So they scramble to find other ways to reward themselves. One woman I know saves her spare change up for an annual weekend retreat at a country inn, with nothing to do there but read, eat, and sleep. Another simply buys herself fresh flowers when she needs recharging. And more than a few have told me that most days it's enough reward to simply gaze at their napping babies, or watch at the door as their older ones come charging home for lunch with amazing stories to tell of their morning at school.

Peer support can be a godsend for at-home moms, and, fortunately, support groups are proliferating. There are political advocacy groups like VOW (Voice of Women) and MAW (Mothers Are Women), and social/educational organizations like the National Association of Mothers' Centers and FEMALE (Formerly Employed Mothers At the Leading Edge), many of which have chapters in cities across North America. (See Resources, page 219.) Community centres, churches, and family service agencies can also provide social and educational support, in both urban and rural areas. For shut-ins with modems, the Internet provides global relief, in the form of life-saving advice, contacts, and vast networking resources. The World Wide Web is a twenty-four-hour social and intellectual hotline for anyone with the technology, the time, and the patience to navigate the wires.

Some great wisdom and howling humour gets shared over the wires, often in the early hours before dawn when the house is quiet and the laundry done. Lea Gust, a twenty-nine-year-old mom from Oregon, posted this 1:35 a.m. message to our e-mail group, in response to another member's cry for help:

> Take heart. I think we all feel this way, at times, which is why we seek out the kinships of others like ourselves. Not many people know the sacrifice of giving up your career for your children or giving up a great double income for a mediocre single one or going from intimate, philosophical or political conversations with your partner to elated discussions of the baby's latest bowel movement! It's not always easy. It's not always fun and we sometimes question our decisions, but know that it is the right one and that feeling unhappy about it isn't a crime and that there are women out here who know exactly what you are going through.

Most stay-at-home moms know, however, that the line between blessing and curse can be a fine one. A full-scale retreat from the work world can spell a dangerous brand of dependence for women — whether it's dependence on a partner or on the welfare system. When a marriage ends, financial dependence can do terrible damage to us and our families. The statistics on single mothers and their children living in poverty are well documented, and what they add up to is this: There may be joy and meaning in home-making, but there's no security.

Even the most affluent wife is at risk, if she has depended on her husband too much and for too long. In divorce court, she will be ordered to make herself financially independent, and do it fast. In most states and provinces, spousal support payments last just a few years, after which the ex-wife will have to earn her own living. Try doing this at age forty-five, or fifty-five, with outdated training, rusty skills, and no self-confidence. If that formerly affluent wife is lucky, she'll be able to sell off what remains of her family assets and live out her life on radically reduced means. Add to her financial trials the humiliation of watching her husband continue to thrive at work, often with a new, younger woman at his side, and you're looking at a very bleak end to what may have started as an "ideal" married life. We must not let this happen to us.

That doesn't mean we ought to discount the value of spending time at home with our children. It just means we dare not lose sight, while we're home, of our future prospects for security and happiness. We will look for opportunities to keep one finger on work while we've got our hands full at home, but, if we agree with Penelope Leach that the interests of our children come first, we'll be careful not to let that equation get turned around. This means seeking compromises that favour our kids, not our jobs, because if we do our planning and keep some perspective, we can always get another job. We only have one chance, though, to get it right with the kids.

The logic of this is clear, once you pull back from work long enough to think about it. The problem is that the logic most of us use at work runs on entirely different principles, and compromise just isn't part of that thinking. Nor is delayed gratification. Some would blame feminists for skewing the value system, making us greedy for the kind of power and position that was denied us for so long. Others suggest there's a larger, generational bias operating here, one that affects men as well as women. It's the boomer bias: our gimme-gimme approach to life, which makes us vulnerable to a consuming passion in our careers and makes it feel like punishment to take time out to care for children. Once we leap onto that fast track at work, it's very easy to come up with good reasons not to leave it for anything, or anyone. Our employers and colleagues reinforce such a choice. In fact, our whole society endorses it.

So what does this say about our society's commitment to children? That's precisely the problem, says Penelope Leach, who prefers to denounce society rather than pick on individual parents. "We leave parents the responsibility for children's well-being and happiness," she writes, "but do we also empower them to ensure it?" The answer, of course, is no. All the power is at work, and the norm is to stay there from 9:00 to 5:00, or longer, if you plan to make anything of yourself. The irony is that it wouldn't take much to tip the scales back towards children — and if we make ourselves heard and apply some pressure, we can bring about such a change. If our society broadly endorsed 7:00–3:00 shifts for working parents of school-age children, for example, think of all the young people who wouldn't have to come home to an empty house. And if time-out for childcare was regarded by employers, not as an inconvenience to them but as a social necessity, think of all the parents who'd happily retreat from work in order to invest some serious time in their families, knowing they could return to their jobs with impunity when they and their children were ready.

ADOLESCENCE: THE BIG SURPRISE

My mother used to tell her daughters that we should have the kinds of careers we could "fall back on" when our kids started school. This was not a unique piece of advice; it was the theme song played by a generation of mothers coaching a generation of career-oriented daughters. Take the time out when they're little, they told us. They're not little for long — blink, and they're gone.

I don't think our mothers meant any harm by this advice. How could they know it wouldn't work? Most moms of 1950s and '60s vintage were in it for the long haul — mothering, that is. "Falling back" on a career must have struck them as a lovely way out of a rather dreary life, something they might have done if they'd planned things right — if they'd had a career to start with, and had the support of their husbands to go back to it. In those days, that was a tall order. Of course, there were a few women back then who went back to work to make something of their college degrees, but most of them did so when their kids were not only at school but able to make their own lunches and walk there. These days, a young mother's career track looks a lot different. It looks much more like her husband's career track, which is what we fought for and what our mothers wholeheartedly endorsed, believing their daughters deserved the chance to achieve great things. After all, the world was to be not only their sons' oyster, but ours too.

It took me more than a decade of full-out dedication to both my career and my children to discover that oysters are vastly overrated. "Great things" can't be accomplished at work when you're constantly feeling distracted and guilty

> **There aren't any win-win solutions. Some compromises are happier than others . . . the ones we should aim for recognize that both parenting and working are lifelong commitments . . .**

about what's happening at home. As a result, the child-rearing years *do not* fly by; they're a painstaking passage through an emotional minefield. When you're in the middle of it, it looks as though it goes on forever. There are times when you feel that if you could channel all that distraction time into productive work time, you'd be able to run Microsoft. There are times when you wish you *could* blink and the kids would be gone. But no such luck. They're with us for a good, long while, and life with them gets harder — much harder — before it gets easier. This is a big surprise to working parents. In fact, the rigours of adolescence come as a downright shock to most of us: fifteen years after maternity leave, and we're still sleep deprived!

With the wisdom of hindsight, I can now say I'm glad that I didn't heed Mom's advice about staying home with my precious little ones. Hunkering down at work during those early years was relatively painless — my children's lives were still uncomplicated, and childcare was quite easy to delegate. Though it was torture to part with my babies some mornings, there were other times when leaving for work was as good as taking off for Hawaii. After a weekend spent feeding, cleaning, running, nursing flus, and feeding and cleaning and running some more, it was sheer luxury to park myself at my quiet, orderly little desk on a Monday morning, with interesting work to do and smart people to talk with. Despite the odd tug of guilt and the drag of fatigue, I counted myself lucky to be there, knowing that my kids were safe in the hands of a loving and capable woman who, similarly, counted herself lucky to have a job in my home. This really wasn't such a bad set-up — especially as it allowed me to spend a great deal of time during my most energetic years building work skills and honing my career network so that I could pull back later without committing professional suicide. I could take some serious time off, then restart my career from home, remaining available to pre-teen kids whose lives were becoming too complex for a hired caregiver to be much help.

I didn't think of this as a strategy back then; I had no idea when I was in my thirties that a "pull-back" was in store for my forties. But in retrospect, I'd have to say it worked out rather well for me, and might even make a good strategy for others. It fits into the "sequencing" philosophy of work which I unwittingly adopted several years before it became trendy (more on sequencing in Chapter Six). It's not perfect, but it's certainly more realistic than that old fall-back scheme promoted by our mothers, who had no idea how hard it would be to return to a career that never had a chance to get off the ground in the first place. Marg Petersen's experience, detailed in the Ex-File on page 168, illustrates the heartaches of a failed fall-back.

There aren't any win-win solutions: no childcare or stay-home or back-to-work strategies that are anything but a compromise. Some compromises are happier than others, however, and the ones we should aim for recognize that both parenting and working are lifelong commitments. We should not have to give up one for the benefit of the other — though there are times when we are called on to invest here, to withdraw there. Finding a rhythm that works for us and our children is the key, because it takes happy parents to raise happy kids. Unfortunately, our work-first society does not promote such a rhythm. It more often promotes a choice: your kids or your career. Not both. The injustice of this hits women hardest, because we're still the ones who shoulder the main burden of that choice. And of course it hits children, especially older children whose need for support and patience and tough love peaks just when their parents are peaking in their careers — or trying to.

Oh, yes: Adolescence is the wrench in our machine. And it's a huge wrench. More than three-quarters of American children between the ages of fourteen and seventeen have working mothers, according to a 1995 *Wall Street Journal* survey. Even if some of those moms work early shifts and a few of the dads stay home, that's still a huge number of teenagers who are home alone after school. Juliet Schor, a Harvard economist and author of *The Overworked American*, estimates that between 1960 and 1986, the amount of time parents were able to spend with their children declined by ten to twelve hours a week. More than seven million North American children are now home alone for parts of each day, most of them adolescents who are too old for babysitters, but too young to be trusted.

Averting disaster is one good reason to spend more time at home with our kids — but it's not the only one. There is also great potential for gratification with older children, if we're there to reap it. Early dalliances in scribbling or tumbling or dress-up drama can suddenly bloom into passions for art or gymnastics or theatre, for which parental support is not only nice but essential. When kids are little, much of their lives can be orchestrated — even from a distance, while you work. When they approach adolescence, great opportunities in parenting crop up at the most inconvenient times — at dawn in a hockey arena, mid-morning at the back of a classroom, midday in a concert hall, or before dinner on a soccer field. A police officer, speaking to parents assembled at our neighbourhood school one evening, put it succinctly: "The kid who stays out of trouble is the one wearing the team jacket," he said, and a lot of us squirmed. To be on a team, and to stick with it through adolescence, takes time — almost as much for the parent as for the child.

Spending time on evenings and weekends to support my children's activities is easy compared with the challenge of monitoring their inactivity in those deadly afternoon hours. This is the ulcer-making time for working moms. For at-home moms, on the other hand, this is payback time — when idle chatter about school friends or weekend plans can suddenly, mysteriously, reveal some nugget of truth that one simply has to be there to catch. (The nuggets never come out at your convenience.) Being there can mean close encounters with your kids' friends, opportunities to observe interactions, and rarer opportunities to participate in them.

When you're around, and they're around, openings tend to *just happen*. In the years when I was working long hours at an office, my kids often went to their friends' houses after school — they seemed to congregate in the homes where the moms were. Perhaps this was because those were the homes with the fullest fridges, or the home-made cookies, or the best prospects for a ride back to our house at dinner time. Or perhaps they sensed those were the homes with a pulse — a high emotional thermostat. I don't know. But I do know I envied those at-home moms, and suffered guilt for not being one.

> In the years when I was working long hours my kids often went to their friends' houses after school . . . perhaps because those were the homes with the fullest fridges . . .

You'd have to go looking really hard to find guilt among at-home moms. Though you will find regrets, frustrations, and insecurities, there's almost always a glowing sense of pride where the children are concerned. This pride doesn't often find public expression, because these mothers know they only gain enemies by talking about how enormously important and satisfying their at-home work is. So they save it for private moments, when they talk among themselves. I've seen this countless times among the women I've interviewed and observed for this book. When given a safe place to emerge, the pride of the at-home mom is nothing short of fierce — far fiercer than anything I've observed among successful working women.

The source of this pride is the conviction shared by stay-at-home moms that they're doing the right thing, for themselves and their kids. Some would go farther, believing they're doing the right thing, period. Changing the world, one diaper at a time, is how a friend of mine puts it. Although I take her point, I prefer a more modest view — one that recognizes a world of diversity in working and parenting styles but puts the at-home choice up there with the best of them. This was eloquently expressed to me by Charmayne Bischel, a middle-aged Oregon homemaker and computer whiz, and host of the popular Web site *Charmayne's Home Sweet Web Home*. For her, being home for her three kids after school — from nursery right through secondary — was the most exciting way Charmayne could imagine spending her time.

> They had so much to share about what had happened during the day. It was the perfect moment for me to give them some help or guidance or comfort or praise for an event — while it was still fresh in their minds. We would sit down, often with a refreshment, and talk, or listen to each other. I can't imagine them having that same enthusiasm and desire to talk and share their day with a parent after going to a day care, babysitter, or whatever after school. Nor can I imagine a tired parent who still has to cook (a well-balanced meal?) and do many other necessary chores having a great deal of enthusiasm for listening to and sharing with the child.

Charmayne could rely on her husband's income as a doctor to support her choice to stay home. She recognizes that the same choice is much harder for young parents to make today, and many simply can't manage it. "I would not want anyone to think that I am totally discouraging working mothers," she insists.

While we must focus on our children, we must still be certain to satisfy our own emotional needs as well. I do not think that a mother who stays home with the kids, while all the time wishing she were working, is being true to either the kids or herself. And you know what? I think that the kids — even at a fairly young age — know, at some level, where her heart is. If she is able to balance both her job and her family in an emotionally healthy manner, more power to her! I know there are many women who are able to do this. I did not feel I was one of them.

If Charmayne has a single answer to this multifaceted question, it's this: Be honest. And I would add a footnote to that (torn from the Boy Scout manual): Be prepared. Specifically, be prepared for the long human childhood. Understand from the outset that your child cannot be neatly downscaled to second priority the moment you decide to put your career back on track. That way, you'll spare yourself a very big surprise: that raising kids does not get easier with the passing of years, but harder, and that the penalty for doing a poor job gets a lot stiffer.

LIKE MOTHER, UNLIKE DAUGHTER

It is endlessly fascinating to watch the ball bounce from one generation to the next. How much of what we strive for and achieve is the result of our mothers' strivings, and failings? Letty Cottin Pogrebin, pioneer American feminist and author, noted this in her latest book, *Getting Over Getting Older*.

It was easy for my generation: most of our mothers didn't "do" anything, so whatever we did was more. Since my mother had to go to work to help support her family, she never went beyond the eighth grade. Just graduating from high school, never mind college, put me in another world.

But today, some young women need two graduate degrees to outdistance their mothers, who are lawyers, doctors and corporate executives. With such a tall order, it's no wonder so many kids have opted out of elite careers.

But there may be a more obvious reason why the "kids" have opted out, and Charmayne Bischel puts her finger on it: "In my own childhood," Charmayne told me, "my mother began working out of the home when I was supposedly old enough to come home to an empty house and take care of myself for awhile. I vividly recall walking into that empty house — how quiet it was."

You could say Charmayne has outdistanced her mom by opting out of the race. And in this, the Portland grandmother is very much like her much younger counterparts — all those rebellious Gen-X daughters of 1970s career women. Rachel LeGrand is one such rebel. Rachel, twenty-seven, lives in Mill Valley, California, with her husband Marty and their two-year-old daughter, Amanda. She worked briefly as an architect until Amanda arrived, but has no intention of going back into that field. Making buildings didn't turn out to be her calling. She plans to have more children, and aims to home-school them right through the secondary grades. She is also training to be a La Leche League leader, and dreams of becoming a midwife one day, which she describes as "the ultimate feminist profession." Rachel's mom is also a feminist — of the old school. She's a practising attorney — "a wonderwoman from the seventies' feminist movement" in Rachel's words:

> Since she felt perfectly comfortable leaving me in childcare from ten months on so that she could become a lawyer, she thinks that I am crazy and goalless to stay at home when I have a career waiting for me in architecture — a male-ego-dominated field, if ever there was one. I try to explain to her that I have a different vision and understanding of feminism. I have respect for what I do, both in and out of my home. I

am not standing still. Sometimes I feel defensive about my choice to stay at home — isn't the fact that it is my choice the salient point? Sometimes I get very upset when other at-home moms I know bad-mouth the feminist movement, although they do have some valid points. Sometimes I get very sad at the divisiveness that the media, and perhaps some extremists, have created between the "stay-at-homers" and the "income producers." It's mostly semantics — we do not stay at home very often. I find staying at home very isolating and crazy-making. Amanda and I lead rather public lives.

We take whatever lessons we can from our mothers, and move on. We become the new pioneers, and our mothers reluctantly concede that it is now our turn. At least, that's what mothers are supposed to do, according to the bouncing-ball theory of social evolution. But it's different for women in these latter years of the century. Our mothers, our older sisters, and many of us fought long and hard to break free of the centuries-old patriarchal bonds that kept women safely in their homes, far from the spheres of power. It is painfully hard to concede, before many of the returns are even in, that the battle might have been misguided — that a correction might already be due. For Rachel's mother, seeing her daughter *choose* to stay home must have been like watching her walk back into the shackles. But for Rachel, this was the ultimate empowerment, and eventually her mother grew comfortable with that choice. Lately, mother and daughter have been talking about starting a business together — a family-friendly storefront operation with a place for Rachel's children to play.

The great feminist revolution of the mid–twentieth century has been triumphant in many ways, but it's not over. Many feminists today want desperately to get beyond their mothers' brand of empowerment, which meant freedom to "succeed" at the expense of their children. What this next generation wants is empowerment that embraces children. Success, to the younger women, is lifelong fulfilment that includes making a home, raising a family, being there for friends, *and* working in their chosen field — if not all at the same time. And if working in their chosen field does not allow that kind of diversity, they're prepared to leave the field, to make a better choice.

This might look like a backlash against feminism. But it can as easily be seen as a new variation on the same theme. Many of the young women I interviewed do consider themselves part of the movement. Significantly, a number of them told me that their seminal moment as a feminist was the birth of their first child. This is what made them proudest to be women, what made them feel powerfully and naturally connected to society and to history. Their mothers must have had the same feeling on being ushered, for the first time, into a boardroom.

> **Success, to the younger women, is a lifelong fulfilment that includes making a home, raising a family, being there for friends *and* working in their chosen field.**

Is this the start of feminism's third wave? Many of the women I've talked to would like to think so. The first wave of feminists fought the pre–World War I battle for civic equality, and the second wave struggled towards reproductive rights and workplace equity. These third-wave feminists will not rest until all women's work — from childcare to quilting to changing the world — finds just reward in our society. Kimberly Patterson, a thirty-nine-year-old at-home mom from Maryland, makes this case for feminism's future:

> I am upset, sometimes, with the idea that women now have "more important things to do" than waste their time with "women's work." Worrying about vacuum coils and drip pans is just as important as car tune-ups. But sometimes it seems that a woman working on a car is seen as doing her part to advance feminism while a woman taking care of her refrigerator is seen as trapped in a mindless world of drudgery — just because the car is part of a *man's* world and the refrigerator is a part of a *woman's*. I think it is all *human* work and I

want the value of it *all* to be recognized. I want staying at home to raise children — and to do housework, and to make the house beautiful with decorative arts and interior design — to be seen as such a valuable part of the human endeavour that no one blinks when it is a man who chooses to stay at home to do it.

There is no neat demographic slot in which to neatly file these "third-wave" feminists. They are young and old, affluent and barely scratching by. Of those who stay home full-time, very few do so without having some kind of paid work they can do from there. Of those who work full-time, most have figured out a way to do so flexibly, through creative negotiation at work and cooperation at home, so that they can find the time they need to raise their children. But what binds all of these women together is the fact of having opted out of the old work model, departing the fast track and all its work-first values. Having come home from the "other side," and having made compromises to get there, they are now clear and articulate about their home-centric ideals.

Anne McKerricher is typical. She calls "women's work" her calling, and is unapologetic about having left a lucrative career in the insurance industry to heed it. Fifteen years ago, and pregnant, she walked away from what most of us would consider a plum job — the most senior position held by any female employee of her company in all of Canada. She and her husband moved, soon afterwards, to a small island off the B.C. coast, a locale that made returning to her career impractical at best. Now forty-five, Anne does a great variety of unpaid work — on school advisory councils, for her political riding association, and on the Boy Scouts' regional executive — and though she thrives on this kind of work, she is proud to call home-making her forte. She has not only learned to live with the necessary compromises, but is grateful for having had the chance.

In many ways I feel that my household resembles the stereotypes of the 1950s, except that we live in the country, not the suburbs. I have made sure that my son's dentist and doctor are women, but I do sometimes worry about the image of women he sees as represented by me. However, I decided that in the final analysis this was my job. My husband works in a stressful job and he is the person who brings the money in. I do the best I can to provide an enriched and beautiful environment with well-cooked meals. That is my job. Sometimes it is boring, it doesn't have the romance of my former high-powered career, but I do find it rewarding most of the time.

HOME: THE LARGER MEANING

"Home" to these women means far more than the roof over their heads. Home is where they measure their own vital signs, through relationships with the most important people in their lives. All of these women have children, but making your home the centre point of your life — a nourishing, comforting, and comfortable place to be — is no less important for those without children, or without a partner. That's because home is really about community, and its inhabitants may be bonded by blood, or geography, or matters of spirit and heart. This larger meaning of home is what economist Shirley Burggraf describes as "the civilized context for human life." And though it is certainly possible to create such a context at work, few of us have that opportunity. Mostly, we work to bring bread home to put on our tables, and once home, we have to work much harder to create the context in which we can fully express ourselves as humans.

That women should be empowered to do this "homework," to do it proudly and well — not in the rushed and half-hearted manner that comes of doing it in our spare time — is precisely what third-wave feminists are fighting for. Author Anne Roiphe calls this third wave "humanist feminism," and since the 1996 release of her book *Fruitful: A Real Mother in the Modern World*, she has been blazing a trail for women of all ages to follow. Roiphe, a grandmother and long-standing feminist, has picked up where Betty Friedan, the other great feminist grandmother, left off. Fifteen years ago, Friedan wrote a book called *Second Stage*, which put forward an agenda for a balanced kind of equality that recognized the rights and needs of women to fulfil nurturing roles within their families and communities. Friedan may have been ahead of her time with that book, or she may have been naive to believe that the strident second-wave feminists of the day would care to accommodate her broad social agenda. In any case, Friedan's voice was drowned out by younger, noisier feminists such as Ellen Willis and Susan Faludi — gender warriors who would have none of this back-to-the-family business. To them, home was the caste system from which modern women had only just broken free.

The third wave is bound to ignite lots more sparks before it is considered a legitimate response to the working woman's dilemma. For one thing, a good many working women don't find themselves in any kind of dilemma — apart from the one created by people like me who seem to have a guilt-making effect on them. (That was never my intention. Life for working women is hard enough without having to suffer guilt on top of it.) Spared such guilt, many career-minded women are perfectly happy with what liberation has done for them. And they don't appreciate having to duck flying platitudes about home sweet home, which is perfectly understandable. No matter what wave we're talking about, feminism is still feminism, and the core value of the movement is to celebrate each woman's right to make informed and dignified choices for herself. To threaten that value is to push a very large, very hot button — which I suppose I did, unwittingly, with my "Superwoman Goes Home" article. I certainly pushed a hot one for Margaret Wente, business editor of *The Globe and Mail*. A few weeks after my cover story hit news stands across the country, Wente published a frothing editorial titled, aptly, "They'll never go home."

"Processed food, refrigerators, microwave ovens and wash-and-wear fabrics have altered our world as profoundly as the automobile or the microchip," wrote Wente, after detailing the contrast between our no-sweat home lives and the labour-intensive lot of our grandmothers.

Today, any family can manage home-maintenance chores in an hour or two a day, and the only time it makes sense for a parent to stay home is when the kids are young. (Technology is not likely to abolish the need for parents.)

There are entire industries devoted to maintaining the illusion that homemaking is still a fulltime job. Idle housewives can take their pick of dozens of made-up arts and crafts, from wreathmaking to decoupage. But it's all pretend. The housewife's job as we've known it for hundreds of years is gone for good — and good riddance. That's the real reason why women have gone out to work, and why they'll never go home again.

Another country heard from, and an important point taken. We will never go home again to a life of domination by husbands and sons, scrub brushes and iceboxes. Nor does our embrace of home preclude any possible brush with commerce, culture, politics, power, or worldly pleasure. Home, according to the third-wave definition, is not a retreat from life, but the base from which a whole life springs. This is nothing new. People have always needed a home base. What is new is the acknowledgement that our society, through its intense focus on work over recent decades, has corroded that base: It's starting to crumble and requires our immediate attention. That's where we need to do some hard work — and not just because we miss our homely comforts, but because when we lose our base, it becomes much harder to do good work out there in the world.

The work that the stay-at-home moms are doing is a vital corrective for our society. It's not something everyone can or should do. But those who have made the choice to stay home, and made the career sacrifices that go with it, deserve recognition for their courage and for their very expensive investment of time. They are trying, in the most unfashionable and politically incorrect way, to right an imbalance that most of us prefer not to think about — and though they're doing it quietly, inside their homes, for their own families, the repercussions will ultimately benefit all of us. Slowly but surely, they are toppling the old superwoman ideal, and bringing common sense back to the family-values debate.

EX-FILE | *Secretary with a Vengeance*

NAME: Margaret Petersen
EX: Stay-at-home mom
CURRENT: Secretary
RÉSUMÉ HIGHLIGHTS: Business college certificate; several years of secretarial work
PERSONAL: Married; three children, 19 to 28; one grandchild

BACKGROUND: When I originally decided to stay at home, when our first child was born, I had absolutely no qualms about my decision. I believed, and still do, that it was the best solution to the child-rearing "problem" both for myself and for the child. I had never even dreamed that it might be difficult to return to the workforce later. Certainly, many women of the previous generation had done exactly that without any terrible problems. I had two years of a college education and felt that that would put me in a good position. I had strong secretarial skills — they were documented by previous employers. I never even considered that staying home to bring up children was like falling off the face of the earth, but it was, and I don't know that I've ever really returned.

There are those who have quite callously suggested that I should have known — that I should have somehow prepared myself for all the changes that would take place in the intervening years. But those years, especially the eighties, took a lot of people by surprise: the sudden decline of the economy, high unemployment, the fact that you had to have computer skills to get any kind of decent job. (Personal computers barely existed when I had my first child.) Adding to this pressure was the tendency of many new mothers not to leave the workforce as we older ones did, which caused a glut in the workforce, especially for traditional women's jobs. In previous generations, pregnant women left positions open for older women to return to. This is not to suggest that it *should* be this way. I certainly understand and respect those who made different choices, and I now understand how the workplace rewards those choices and penalizes those of us who choose to interrupt our careers for motherhood.

I have a very good friend who is fifteen years my senior. Her experience was vastly different from mine. When her children graduated from high school, she easily found a job as an assistant librarian, although she hadn't used those skills for all the years she was at home. That was the norm for her peers. It all changed for my peer group, and this continues to be the reality: that anyone who becomes a stay-at-home mom is putting herself at great risk. She may feel that life is about risk and that the benefits to children are so great that it is worth the risk — in fact, this is how I feel at the end of the day, and it's the reason I don't have major regrets. On the other hand, if I could have predicted how society would change, I'd have done more while I was at home to upgrade my skills and improve my job prospects for later.

ODD JOBS: I took my first job when our eldest child was in high school. It was a night job in the distribution department of a newspaper — basically grunt work at slave wages, but it fit the family schedule and it was a pay cheque. I believed it would be a viable re-entrance to the workplace, but I was proven wrong. I worked there for five years and, feeling that I was getting too old for that kind of work, I quit — big mistake! — and began looking for more suitable work in my field (secretarial).

I had been taking computer classes, and felt I was prepared. However, employers thought otherwise. At forty-two, I was "too old" for them, and with the very sexist attitudes that are still prevalent in our society — that a front desk receptionist must be pert, pretty, and, most of all, young — I had little chance of finding a job.

I spent the better part of a year looking and finally wound up as a clerk in a convenience store. I worked there for two years and finally found a secretarial job that I liked and paid well. I thought I was set, but once again, the economy stepped in and dealt a bitter blow. Cuts in higher education affected all businesses here in Corvallis, a college town. My company went under, and I was once again unemployed. This time, it went on for five years.

DESPAIR: Those years were a very traumatic time for myself and for my family who were extremely supportive but couldn't do anything about my situation. Our eldest had just begun his second year of college, his brother was finishing high school, and his little sister was still in elementary. Even though both boys had scholarships, finances were very tight. We had always thought that by this time in our lives, I would be working full-time and helping to contribute. I found my inability to do so extremely devastating personally and it was crippling financially. Debts piled up, and my frustration eventually led to severe depression and thoughts of suicide.

Until I became unemployed myself, I had no idea of the frustration and downright helplessness that one can feel in that situation. People are always saying, "If you want to work, you *will* find it." It's a nice sentiment and there are some who really believe it, but I believe that for most it is simply a way of negating the very real problem of unemployment and discrediting those who find themselves there. After all, if my experiences are to be believed (somewhat educated, with marketable skills and good references and tons of motivation, yet still not finding employment), then others would be forced to admit that they too could be in such a situation. And that is *not* something a lot of people would like to face. Much easier and more comfortable to simply believe that those who are unemployed are lazy and/or unskilled.

THE SOLUTION: During this time, I was "saved" by rediscovering an interest in writing. I concentrated on what I *could* do and tried to ignore the rest. It wasn't easy and I frequently failed, but I held to the belief that if one doesn't do what one loves, then there can be no possibility of succeeding at it. Simply *wishing* that you'd followed your dreams doesn't cut it. Having said that, I don't expect success to include making a lot of money at writing. Actually, I've made nothing at writing, yet. But I can afford to keep trying because I've found a secretarial job that I like — finally!

Yes, I know, I am a very peculiar sort. I actually *like* secretarial work. There is something in me that enjoys the attention to detail, and the joy that helping others gives me, as well as organizing and tracking data. I work for an Internet provider and I do believe that my being in the front office gives some other "older" people the confidence that they too can do it — get connected, that is. And since I have only recently gotten connected myself, I have some understanding of what these people don't know and what they need to know, and how to answer their questions without being condescending.

We still have unbelievable debts that, some days, I despair of ever paying off before my husband retires. And we still have our daughter to help through college. (She is in her first year and has terrific potential.) So, at a time when we expected to be somewhat financially secure, we find ourselves the complete opposite. However, we *will* succeed in our primary goal — that of giving our children the best start in life that we can.

TAKE-OUT WISDOM: I would advise extreme caution when considering becoming a stay-at-home mom. However, having said that, I would also suggest that being a stay-at-home mom is the absolutely *most* rewarding job there is. Even if I had known how brutal my return to work would be, I would still have chosen what I did. I have counselled my own kids to stay at home if they choose to, but have urged them to be aware of the risks and to make every effort to stay connected to their work in some way during those years at home. If I had known how terribly difficult it was going to be for me, I would have taken courses sooner and I would have been less willing to take "get-by" jobs.

However, I can excuse myself to some degree because, well, who could have predicted what these last twenty years would bring? Sometimes, it really doesn't matter how well you plan. You can't possibly know exactly what societal, economic, or personal changes (such as divorce) might be in the wings. You can only do your best at finding work that feels productive to you, and hope that society will not turn its back on you for making a choice to slow down in your outside work for a number of years so that you can do your inside work, at home, with your family. Our society needs us for this work, and should recognize it as such and respect those who do it. Maybe one day it will.

 **CHECK |**
| *Your Partner's Support*

1. **RATE YOUR SIGNIFICANT OTHER**

   This quiz was written by Nancy Baker Fowler, a member of my feminist moms' e-mail group. She posted it on the list for fun, and insists it be taken that way. Your SO's (significant other's) score will give a rough measure of the value he puts on household work — and his willingness to participate in it. Several members of the group reported that the quiz prompted spirited discussion and lit more than a few fires. One member described an emotionally charged predawn discussion with her SO on the topic of priorities and mutual respect, with both parties feeling resolved and affectionate at the end. Another member, on seeing her husband score way down in the SO dumps, posted this message:

Well, I am not even going to add up these measly points. Sounds like I am married to a schmuck, huh! However, I am going to counterpoint: I never scrub grout. We hired a cleaning person to come in and mop the floors, etc., and it saved our marriage. The laundry, along with wet towels (after a shower) are things our cleaner can't do, and they still get to me. But I let go of a lot of it, because, hey, I still love the guy.

The Quiz

The baby needs to be changed. Your SO:
   a) says "Honey the baby needs to be changed."
   b) says "I'm changing the baby. Where are the diapers/wipes/changing pad?"
   c) changes the baby.
   d) notices that it is bedtime. Gives the baby a bath, puts on pjs and clean diaper and brings her to you to say goodnight.

You put the clean laundry on the stairs. Your SO:
   a) steps over it.
   b) takes it upstairs and dumps it on the bed.
   c) takes it upstairs and puts it away.
   d) takes it upstairs and while he is putting it away, reorganizes all the drawers and closets.

You finish a meal. Your SO:
   a) gets up and walks away.
   b) gets up and puts the dishes on the counter above the dishwasher, because SO couldn't tell if the dishes in the dishwasher were clean or dirty.
   c) gets up and loads the dishwasher (emptying it if the dishes are clean).
   d) gets up and loads up the dishwasher, scrubs all the pots and pans, wipes down the counters and sweeps and mops the floor.

SO clogs up the toilet before leaving for work. Your SO:
   a) leaves it for you to deal with.
   b) plunges it and gets it "mostly" unclogged.
   c) clears the clog and cleans up the mess.
   d) clears the clog, cleans up the mess, washes the floor, scrubs out the tub and cleans the grout.

You call SO at work to pick up milk on the way home. Your SO:
   a) calls back 5 min later and says "Did you just call me?"
   b) comes home without the milk, opens the fridge and says "we're out of milk."
   c) picks up the milk.
   d) picks up the milk and decides to do the week's grocery shopping to save you a trip.

You call SO to find out what time to expect SO home from work. SO says 6:30.
   a) SO shows up at 7:30.
   b) you call SO at 6:30 and SO says " I'm leaving now."
   c) SO shows up at 6:30.
   d) SO shows up at 5:30 because it sounded like you were having a bad day and SO picked up dinner on the way home.

Score the following way for each answer:
   a)   1 point
   b)   2 points
   c)   3 points
   d)   4 points

RESULTS:

   6 – 9 points: Your significant other needs to be more significant around the house.

10 – 14 points: Sounds like your SO is trying.

15 – 19 points: SO is pulling his weight.

20 – 24 points: Where did you find your SO????? And can I have one?? :-)

2. CAN WE TALK?

If you are considering a major change at work, you'll need the support of the people at home. It sounds obvious, but many of us put off conversations we fear might be emotionally loaded. It is often easier to talk to colleagues and supervisors at work than to have that essential heart-to-heart at home. Big mistake. When families are involved, *my* plan has to be *our* plan — if it's going to succeed, long term. Here is a checklist to help you bring your partner into the loop.

❏ I've shared my planning steps with my partner as a way to demonstrate how I've carefully worked out the details; (or: I've asked my partner to work with me on my detailed plan for change).

❏ We've discussed how the quality of our family life is affected by our current work arrangements and lifestyle.

❏ We've discussed what we would like to change in our current situation.

❏ We've discussed our feelings about the kind of family life we'd like to have.

❏ We've discussed each of our goals and roles in fulfilling that vision.

❏ We've discussed the shift in values that may be necessary as we make financial adjustments.

❏ We've discussed how to deal with any power shift that may come with one of us bringing in less income.

❏ We've worked out a household budget and spending plan that we both can agree to.*

❏ We've discussed whether or not my partner might feel added financial pressure, and how we might deal with this.

❏ We've discussed the benefits of the change.

❏ We've discussed how long I anticipate having a changed work schedule.

❏ We've discussed how our long-term financial and professional goals might be affected.

❏ We've discussed our future plans for family growth and change, and how we can achieve (or alter) these.

❏ We've discussed expectations and changes related to household roles (housework, childcare, bill paying, etc.).

❏ To reach mutually agreeable terms, we've made modifications to my plan based on our discussions.

❏ We've reached agreement on a reasonable timeline for change.

❏ We are both committed to doing our best to make our plan work**

See page 214 for budget planning help.

CHECK |
Your Stress Level

1. THE PHYSICAL SIGNS

Stress is a constant in life, like drizzle on a spring day. You can't get rid of it, nor would you want to. But when the rain swells creeks and floods basements — that's when it's time to call for help. Undue stress — the kind that leads to chronic pain, exhaustion, drug and alcohol abuse, depression, or marital breakdown — is your body's way of saying you missed the flood warning, and the damage has been done. The problem is, many of us don't see the warnings in time.

The best way to monitor your stress level is to know your body well. Though each person responds differently, stress takes its toll in fairly predictable ways. The physical signs usually involve muscles, the heart, gastrointestinal (GI) tract, or skin:

Muscles

*Excerpted from the workbook-on-disk, Flex Success: A Proposal Blueprint for Getting a Family-Friendly Work Schedule. Reprinted by permission of Work Options, Inc. Website www.lava.net/workoptions. To order: 1-808-531-9939 in Canada, 1-888-279-FLEX in US.

THE CRISIS: The body's fight-or-flight warning system runs on stress hormones from your adrenal glands. Push the panic button and any or all of your 650 muscles tense up. Heart rate and blood pressure rise, your breathing quickens, and sugars and fats are released into the bloodstream, giving the characteristic power surge that will help you deal with the crisis: lift that car off the pinned child; close that brutal business deal. This is a good thing — unless the tension persists and all those muscles remain primed for action. When the blood flow diminishes, the muscles become starved for oxygen and they stiffen. Muscle-contraction problems most commonly affect the neck and back, with associated pain, immobility, and "tension headaches."

RESPONSE: Anything that keeps muscles pliable — gentle stretching, massage, yoga, swimming — helps reduce neck and back pain. Tension headaches can be relieved by calming baths, breathing exercises, meditation, or aromatherapy. If daily activity is impeded, consult your doctor.

Heart

THE CRISIS: The adrenalin surge that primes your muscles also stresses your heart. This, too, is a good thing — in time of crisis. Arteries dilate, increasing blood flow to your muscles; blood platelets become stickier so that you are less likely to bleed to death if injured. What all this feels like, to you, is a racing heart with seemingly loud, often irregular beats. A day or even a week of this may not harm you, but over the longer term those adrenal hormones coursing too quickly through your system will cause artery walls to scar and pit. Fatty cells can more easily adhere to the pocked surfaces, resulting in narrowed vessels, decreased blood flow, and, eventually, oxygen deprivation to the body. This can lead to chest pain and, in extreme cases, stroke or heart attack. Specialists are increasingly targeting women for heart-disease prevention, because many of us mistakenly believe men are more likely candidates.

RESPONSE: When you feel the onset of cardiac stress — thumping, racing, or irregular heartbeat — deep relaxation techniques such as breathing exercises can be very effective. If you don't feel relief after a few days, see your doctor. Long-term strategies: Include a pleasant, relaxing activity in your daily schedule; prioritize activities to reduce pressure to "do it all."

Gastrointestinal Tract

THE CRISIS: The brain's emotion centres are linked to the abdomen by the vague and sympathetic nerves. When stress strikes, the brain sends its warning through these neurotransmitters which then douse the gastrointestinal (GI) tract with hormones. The GI tract responds in several ways — by going into spasms, slowing down or speeding up, or secreting excess acids. One of the most common results is irritable bowel syndrome, in which the colon works either too quickly or too slowly. This can cause pain, bloating, and bouts of constipation and/or diarrhea. Another stress-induced GI ailment is non-ulcer dyspepsia, or NUD, caused by excess stomach acid. This causes bloating in some and tenderness in others as the stomach fails to properly empty its contents.

RESPONSE: Prescription antispasmodic drugs are often used to regulate irritable colons. Over-the-counter antacids, such as Pepto-Bismol or Mylanta, offer temporary relief from NUD, though prescription medications may be required to promote gastric emptying. Relaxation and diet are equally important for both these conditions. Caffeine, nicotine, and alcohol ought to be limited if not avoided, as they only aggravate a stressed GI tract even more.

Skin

THE CRISIS: Because it's so public, your skin has a nasty habit of both reflecting and aggravating stress problems. The more your skin reacts to stress, the more stressed you are. The fight-or-flight hormone, cortisol, promotes secretion of androgen — a sex hormone that increases oil production and suppresses the immune system, making the skin less resistant to acne-aggravating bacteria. This can cause adolescent-type breakouts on adults. At the same time, a stressed body prioritizes its blood flow, sending the majority of blood to its most vital organs — the brain, heart, and lungs. Suffering from a reduced blood flow, the skin often becomes pale and dehydrated, resulting in the twin plagues of acne and dry, flaky patches. It gets worse for those prone to allergies. Stress can induce the release of histamines, setting off itching, inflammation, rashes, and hives.

RESPONSE: Over-the-counter drying products containing salicylic acid, sulphur, or benzoyl peroxide often help to dry up oily areas. A moisturizer can help alleviate flakiness, while moderate daily aerobic exercise boosts circulation, delivering a healthier flow of blood to the skin. For hives, inflammation, or itching, your doctor may prescribe antihistamines.

Help on the bookshelves:

The Female Stress Syndrome, by Georgina Witkin, Ph.D., Newmarket Press; *It's Not All In Your Head,* by Susan Sedo, M.D., and Henrietta Leonard, HarperCollins; *Why Zebras Don't Get Ulcers*, by Robert M. Sapolsky, Ph.D., W.H. Freeman and Company; *Skin Deep: A Mind/ Body Program for Healthy Skin,* by Ted A. Grossbart, Ph.D., Health Press; *From Stress to Strength: How to Lighten Your Load and Save Your Life*, by Robert S. Eliot, M.D., Bantam.

2. A SOCIAL CURE

"This is the great error of our day in the treatment of the human body, that physicians separate the mind from the body." Socrates wrote that 2,300 years ago, and not much has changed — at least, not in the traditional school of medical science. Fortunately, holistic practitioners are making inroads, drawing connections between emotional distress, physiological stress, and the health of our immune systems. Though we may not be able to prevent diseases such as cancer, arthritis, or multiple sclerosis simply by reducing stress, there is a growing canon of research to show that we do have the power to slow the progress of those diseases. One well-known study showed that women with breast cancer attending a support group had a much longer survival time than a similar group with no such support.

Strengthen your support system, boost your immune system. Simplistic? Or simple wisdom? Ask anyone who has relied on caring friends or family members where they would be without their helpmates. Yet many of us, under the pressure of balancing work and family responsibilities, have cut our social-support lifelines. When we're not at work, we're merely coping. We stay "in touch" with friends, and hope to reconnect more deeply later, when we have the time. Some of us have left best friends and loved ones behind in order to follow our careers to new opportunities in new places. We can't always avoid this; work intervenes, and life changes. But we can do ourselves the favour of recognizing that support lost must be found again. New friends can meet our needs almost as well as old ones, when given the chance — and the time.

Fill out this chart to determine the strength of your support network. Enter a score of "1" in each box if you rely regularly on that person for the type of support described in the column on the far left. Enter "2" if that person reciprocates by coming to you for the same kind of support. Leave the box blank if you can't depend on anyone who fits that category for the type of support described. Put the sum of your numbers in the final column. Then add these subtotals, counting the emotional subtotal twice (it's worth its weight in gold).

TYPE OF SUPPORT	Partner	Relative	Friend	Neighbor	Coworker	Boss	Therapist or Minister	SUBTOTAL	ABOVE 25 You have a healthy support network. You're capable of getting the help you need and of caring for others in return.
EMOTIONAL Someone you can trust with your most intimate thoughts and fears									
SOCIAL Someone with whom you can hang out and share life experiences									**25 OR BELOW** Your social safety net seems to have some holes in it. If you don't fill them in, isolation could eventually take a toll on your health.
INFORMATIONAL Someone you can ask for advice on major decisions									
PRACTICAL Someone who will help you out in a pinch									

_____ **TOTAL**

Reprinted with permission from HEALTH © 1997.

SIX

Five Strategies for Reworking Your Life

No more "that was then, this is now." It's time to move on to the future — *your* future — which is the real challenge of this book. Is it possible to put all the lessons of Chapters One through Five together and find, therein, the solution to every woman's dilemma at work?

There is no easy solution, I promise you that. On the other hand, there are more openings for change now than any of us could have guessed at a few years ago when all the rules about "career success" seemed so rigidly prescribed. This is the great opportunity of today: to find our own definition of success, which is the silver lining in the dark cloud of social upheaval that hangs over us. We can see disaster in that cloud if we look for it, but we can also see the glimmer of promise.

THE NEW MODEL OF SUCCESS

In written Chinese, a single character connotes both disaster and opportunity. There's wisdom in that, and we can borrow it to help us take a healthy, holistic view of our futures. When we stop what we're doing and open the blinds, we see millions of people doing just that: stopping, taking stock, tearing up labels that have been defining and confining them for too long. As we learned in Chapter Two, clarity needs its chance to strike. If an unstable economy or a downsizing employer is what it takes to make us pause, this can turn out to be a necessary corrective. Those with courage and imagination will reap gains from such changes, finding a more successful footing in the new economy and the new social order that accompanies it. Rather than fall victim to the changes, these women and men will take their place as renovators of the old work structures.

But there are different ways to renovate, depending on one's idea of what the new structure ought to look like. Depending, in other words, on one's model of success. Do we want a world where greater profits can be made by fewer, braver workers? Where only those who are young, single, and "wired" can win the info-age sweepstakes? Where we're forced to use any and all means to get to the winner's circle, including cleavage power? Are we content to dismantle the obsolete structures but leave the old, work-dominated, male-oriented foundations in place?

Despite all the excitement about the workplace revolution, it is far from clear whether this revolution is going to be good or bad for most women. What will become of those who aren't so brave, or young, or hardy? Nor is it clear what the changes will mean for our families and communities — though many of us fear a very poor result. In her 1997 book, *The Time Bind: When Work Becomes Home and Home Becomes Work*, sociologist Arlie Russell Hochschild issues a potent warning: Many of the changes that appear to reward us in today's innovative workplaces actually undermine us at home. As the management emphasis in recent years has turned from long-term succession to short-term success (where employees are being groomed for maximum performance on *today's* project), the reward system has shifted from security to immediate gratification. In the most innovative companies, work just keeps getting better and better, for those of us who do well at it and who don't mind living for today.

At one firm, where the new Total Quality Management philosophy is in full swing, Hochschild observes a heightened sense of employee morale that makes family time pale by comparison. And she is not only observing executives in action; many of her interview subjects work on the factory floor. Throughout the TQM company, top to bottom, a family feeling is promoted as the key plank in the team-performance philosophy. To this end, teams wearing TQM pins are honoured at "recognition ceremonies," and workers are treated as "internal customers" who are valued just as highly as are the external customers (i.e., clients). This is seductive stuff, notes Hochschild. "How many recognition ceremonies for competent performance are being offered at home? Who is valuing the internal customer there?"

The result is that workers spend more time at work, where all the rewards are, and less time at home, where the conflicts are. This is not quality, says Hochschild. It's poison. And it becomes even more toxic when the word "global" is added to it. In a global market, we are increasingly urged to break through the old barriers — figuratively and geographically. The new corporate world creates virtual neighbourhoods and expects workers to live there. And where is *there?* It is wherever today's task needs to be done. In the information age, high-performance workers are expected to be mobile, and so are their families — if they have them. And they often don't have them for long, because such demands only drive another wedge between ourselves and our familial/emotional/spiritual roots. Without roots, it's hard for a family to thrive.

The popular wisdom says our economy is correcting itself, that the new engines of success are purring once again. But those of us who value our families and communities are obliged to study that correction and be prepared to call it wrong if that's how we see it. If we are truly seeking a correction in the course of our own lives, not just in the engines of our economy, we must use our wits and our hearts to navigate our own course to a better future. For many women, this will mean steering out of the narrow channels prescribed by the male model of success in a work-first society. Our version of "total quality management" will not be about jumping on new bandwagons that only make us work harder. Nor will it be about embracing the new technology only as a means to work longer hours and in more locations. Total quality management, to us, will mean working smarter — working less so we can live more.

Yes, we still want power, respect, and pay equity at work. But we also want time *away* from work to tend to the rest of our lives: time at home, with our families and in our communities. We want, and need, time to rebuild the base that gives context to a civilized human life. That base has become badly eroded by a culture that puts work first but forgets to ask, Why? And at what expense?

So here is the great opportunity for women: By making a commitment to change, and by finding our voice to express that desire, we will ensure that the new blueprint for a working society actually *works* for most of us who live here. Indeed, we've already started making an impact. The voices of women are being heard. We've been welcomed into the new economy because we so clearly belong here, but we are still a long way from equal representation in the boardroom, and therefore a long way from the blueprints of corporate change. Our contributions are being noted, especially in large public companies that are most responsive to media pressure. But even in those companies, our performance is still being measured by somebody else's yardstick, and we're being held back by our lack of numbers. Women hold fewer than 10 per cent of board seats in Fortune 500 companies. Only five per cent of senior managers in those companies are women, up only two percentage points in the last five years. We've made a little progress, but we have serious work still to do.

> **Despite all the excitement about the workplace revolution, it is far from clear whether this revolution is going to be good or bad for most women.**

Of course we don't need to gather in boardrooms to make our mark on the blueprint for social change. We can also gather in mail rooms, or church basements, or kitchens, or all of the above, to fight for our right to live a rich and diverse life. Wherever we're coming from, wherever we're going, the goal is the same: to take charge of our lives and put work in its place.

STRATEGY #1: WORKING LESS

For many of us, a simple solution would do it: a shorter week at work, a longer one at home — accompanied by society's endorsement of such an arrangement as not a step back but a valid evolution of a person's life and career. This would go a long way to curing what most pollsters call the North American epidemic: exhaustion.

Barbara Thurston has embraced such a strategy. She graduated in 1987 with a mathematics degree from Indiana University, and since then has worked in the insurance industry while continuing to upgrade her skills. By 1994 she was married, living in Juneau, Alaska, and holding a $70,000-a-year job as the only actuary in the state's insurance division. The following year she became pregnant, worked right up to her due date, took an eighteen-week maternity leave following the birth of Stuart, then returned to full-time work.

> Over the next couple of months, it became clear to me that this was no way to live — we spent five days a week struggling to survive and looking forward to the weekend, when we ran errands and did housework. So I approached my boss and asked to switch to part time. I really had no idea what she'd say — no one else in the division works part time, and there are not many state employees in general who work part time. I figured the worst that would happen is that she'd say no. She actually said, "Write me a memo explaining what you want to do, how your work will be allocated, and the pros and cons." I worked hard on that memo, and she agreed to let me go part time, which I did in November of '95, when Stuart was ten months old.
>
> It is great. I still toy with the idea of staying home full time, and might some day, but moving to part time has made such a difference in my outlook and in my family's stress level that I can't imagine going back too soon. I'm a big advocate of part-time work, especially for mothers of young children. My productivity per hour is significantly higher than it was

when I was working full time — I accomplish almost as much as I did then. This agrees with what I've seen elsewhere, and should serve to make part-time work more appealing to employers.

There are some drawbacks to working part time. My daycare costs (in a family daycare) are essentially the same as they were when I was working full time. One of the conditions of my contract that hasn't changed is that I need to be able to travel and stay late when necessary. So, by paying for full-time daycare, I reserve the slot in the afternoon for those days when I need it. Also, the hourly rate for daycare is high enough that five hours at the hourly rate is essentially the same as the daily rate. I also find it frustrating because all the parent/child activities, like story time at the library and preschool open gym, are only available in the mornings, probably because little kids nap in the afternoons. So I miss out on all that. I also don't get much in the way of benefits, which isn't that big a problem because I'm covered under my husband's health insurance, but this could be a big problem for others. On balance, for me, it's pretty close to perfect.

A lot of women would agree with Barbara's assessment, but few of us have her resources. So most of us remain overworked and under-rewarded, and it's getting worse all the time. Since 1969, according to Harvard economist Juliet Schor in *The Overworked American*, the average worker has added one month of work time to his or her annual schedule, and the average family has added more than 1,000 hours per year of work. Working mothers are hardest hit, with one study suggesting we work more than eighty hours a week on average, when paid and unpaid duties are combined.

A growing number of women say they would happily trade some income gains for increased off-duty time to attend to family and personal needs, given the chance. In a survey conducted by the New York–based Families and Work Institute, 78 per cent of respondents said they would choose free time over career advancement; 55 per cent of both women and men said they would be less likely "to accept a promotion involving greater responsibility if it meant spending less time with family." More than half of all working women would like more flexibility in their job descriptions and schedules, and as many as one-third of full-time-working women with young children said they would scale back to part-time if they could do so without compromising their benefits or security.

Most women, it seems, would like to take a comfortable middle road. But we don't know how to get there, and in weary frustration we look back at our mothers' lives and grow envious. Though we're proud of what we've achieved, and don't really want to quit, we don't want to keep working either — at least, not this hard. A 1992 *ABC News* poll illuminated the extent of our conflict: 59 per cent of the working women surveyed agreed that "the changes in American life caused by more women working outside the home have been worth making," but 58 per cent nevertheless longed for the days in which women didn't work outside the home.

Does this mean we "want it all?" I don't think so. Most of us would settle for a modest compromise, such as shorter work hours, or more flexible schedules, or having the freedom to take a leave of absence now and then — paid, or partially paid, or even unpaid — without sacrificing long-term security. For many of us, on-site childcare would make the difference between mere survival and true satisfaction on the job. And telecommuting would be ideal for "modem moms" who can handle living in two worlds at once. While such options are increasingly available in today's work world, many companies remain rooted in yesterday's rules.

So, what if you're working for a dinosaur? Pulling back at work can be a deadly mistake if your employer is stuck in the old bottom-line logic. And that's still a lot of employers — particularly the smaller, family-owned firms that do not fall under public scrutiny and tend to be the last to bring in reforms. What's called for is artful and patient negotiation, and to get off on the right foot you've got to do your homework. It might be wise to seek vocational advice, or you might find the resources you need in the bookstores. A number of excellent workbooks and software packages are also available to guide novices through the thorny process of contract negotiation. One of the best tools I've found is the aforementioned program called Flex Success, developed by Honolulu-based consultant Pat Katepoo. Included in her program is advice on how to decide which work option best meets your personal needs, a detailed blueprint to help you negotiate your proposal for change, and strategies to enhance the chances of your proposal being accepted. (See Check, page 176)

The only way to negotiate for shorter or more flexible work time is from a position of strength, and preferably with a back-up plan: "This is what I need, and this is what I'll do if I can't get it." Of course, it helps if you've made yourself valuable at work. Don't even start talking to your employer until you know exactly where you stand, where you'd like to stand, and how you intend to proceed towards that goal. Many of the planning steps outlined in "Strategy #3: Working Flex" (page 193) below, can also be used in your negotiations to work less.

To add your voice to the larger cause, contact the Shorter Work-Time Network. Bruce O'Hara, spokesman for SWT Canada, has a library of resource material available to anyone interested in the campaign. "When almost everyone is stressed out — either by unemployment or by overwork — it's necessary to create a 'Psst, pass it on' movement where a great many people do a little bit each," says O'Hara, who lives on Vancouver Island. Network volunteers are available to make presentations to work groups, clubs, and professional associations in most major Canadian cities. (For details see page 239.)

STRATEGY #2: NOT WORKING

Dropping out is the most radical response to work-induced fatigue, and significant numbers of North American boomers have headed for simple pleasures on a Spartan budget. Though the "Simple Living" movement is likely to remain a fringe affair, the fringe has grown larger and louder in recent years. Juliet Schor says the drop-outs are doing nothing less than staging an in-your-face protest against the American dream — announcing by their exit from the fast track that they are no longer interested in "playing ball." Interviewing hundreds of white-collar drop-outs for her next book, Schor found many common themes. These former executives complained of debilitating stress in their former jobs, of being intellectually and spiritually unsatisfied there, of leaving in order to find new meaning. Many had gotten themselves fired, and moved on to less demanding, lower-paying jobs, with no regrets.

Even to those of us too timid, too sensible, or too broke for such extreme action, the drop-outs' message gives pause for thought. We were raised with the faith that hard labour would eventually bear fruit in the form of affluence, leisure, and happiness. That was, after all, the American dream — the original version. With courage and optimism in the face of the coming Depression, pioneer capitalists such as W. K. Kellogg reduced work hours at their factories, not just to spread more jobs around a needy population, but to help their employees find the time they needed to enjoy their hard-earned wages. But such principles did not last long in a society in which ad-driven consumer lust and its side-kick, easy credit, rapidly overtook "happiness" as the fuel that drove the work engines.

> **While the prospect of a full retreat to the home sounds exactly right to some women, it strikes many others as an invitation to isolation, insecurity, and marital imbalance.**

In the suburbs of North America after the Second World War, everyone was living to work, and working to pay for the new dining-room suite. "Leisure became trivialized, and the serious responsibilities of leisure culture — family and community — were neglected as work became a moral solvent for the results of that neglect," says American historian Benjamin Hunnicutt, one of the authors of the 1996 Iowa City Declaration and a founding father of the Shorter

Work Time movement. "Ask someone who they are and their identity is tied to their work," complains Hunnicutt. Not so, however, on the simple-living fringe, where the old "happiness" message is being heard once again, uttered by voluntarily disenfranchised suburbanites. And though they're small in number, we'd be misguided not to heed them.

The Bible for those who are drawn to the simple-living movement is Vicki Robin and Joe Dominguez's best-seller *Your Money or Your Life*, which charts their own path from six-figure stress to happiness on $6,000 a year. Since the Seattle duo launched the movement with that book in 1992, an entire library has sprung up to offer simple-living inspiration and help. Half the Web sites on the Internet seem to be linked to a simplicity site: try "simple living" on a keyword search.

It seems half the simplicity sites on the Web are also linked to stay-at-home parenting sites, which is not surprising when you consider the financial penalty of staying home. But staying home, like simplicity, will likely remain a minority option — and not only because of the income loss. While the prospect of a full retreat to the home sounds exactly right to some women (especially those who are suffering burn-out at work), it strikes many others as an invitation to isolation, insecurity, and marital imbalance. The truth about staying home is actually much more complicated than that — and much more individual. Many of the women I know who are dedicating themselves full-time to raising families do not feel socially isolated, insecure, or disempowered in the least. This is partly because many of them have partners who support at-home parenting as a family choice. But mostly it's because these women have rejected the social values that would cast them in such dim light. When you no longer allow a job to be the touchstone of your identity, you allow many other things to rush in and fill the void — and I'm not just talking about laundry and soap operas.

This defence of the stay-home choice was made clearly in a discussion group I attended, where the topic of the day was an article in *Working Mother* magazine. This is not the best magazine, I should add, for at-home moms in need of validation. As its title suggests, it is a magazine for moms who work, and regardless of the reasons its readers may have for working (choice, necessity, or the usual combination thereof), *Working Mother* does a great job of framing it as a choice — and the best one at that. While most of the at-home moms in my discussion group respect the magazine's mandate and understand its reasons for promoting working motherhood, they were nevertheless disappointed to see themselves so badly maligned in the February 1997 cover story, "Why It Pays to Keep Working." The subtitle ran: "If you just cut back, argue proponents of the simplicity movement, you can afford to stay home. Here's why they couldn't be more wrong." The author was Lesley Alderman (significantly, she's also a reporter for *Money Magazine*), and her modus operandi was to systematically trash all the reasons a woman could possibly have to stay home and raise children.

Essentially, Alderman's critique of staying home boiled down to this: "Quitting your job, even temporarily, could have serious and irreparable consequences on your long-term earning power and future financial security." The off-work mom will be earning at least 10 per cent less than peers and colleagues on her return to work, wrote Alderman, quoting financial experts. "Even 20 years after they rejoin the work force, reentry women still earn five to seven percent less than their peers with comparable education and experience." The "reentry woman" will also have missed valuable contribution time for income-based retirement savings plans and pensions; she will have compromised the power balance in her marriage ("the more the wife contributes to the family income, the more decision-making power she has"); and her family's future security will be on the line. What if your spouse becomes disabled, or leaves you? And, worse, what if you had to start wearing jeans and sweats all the time? Would you be happy?

The article raised many salient points, but it was perhaps this last one that pushed the women in my discussion group over the edge.

By describing the "psychic price" of having to give up your business suits and silk blouses, *Working Mother* betrayed its bias — first, that the alternative to staying home is an executive job (would a grocery clerk have a hard time giving up her apron?) and second, that full-time parenting has no inherent value that might counterbalance the professional and financial costs. While the wardrobe debate prompted the most laughter in the discussion group — these women considered themselves privileged to be wearing recycled Levi's and T-shirts — it was the *values* debate that really got their blood boiling.

> **Though many of us don't have a choice about whether we work to support our families, we do have choices on how we measure our accomplishments at work and at home.**

This debate springs from a basic disagreement about how we choose to define success. Though many of us don't have a choice about whether we work to support our families, we do have choices on how we measure our accomplishments at work and at home. For some women, success may be measured in the few thousand extra dollars they can earn by avoiding a maternity "disruption." For others, success *is* the disruption. Of all the at-home women I've interviewed, most agree there are risks to staying home, but few would read those risks as: Danger, Do Not Enter! It's more like: Caution, Enter With Care. With some creative risk management, they've found, it is possible to mitigate the financial damages of staying home and get on with doing what's needed there.

In order to weigh the stay-home option with an open mind, it is necessary to navigate out of those narrow channels where success is defined by the workplace, and this is what *Working Mother* was patently not prepared to do. From *WM*'s vantage point, staying home in the nineties does not look much different from staying home in the fifties — a passive acceptance of what the work-first culture expected of working men's wives. But according to the radicalized nineties mom, staying home entails an active decision to trash the old bottom-line thinking. Tearing off her silk blouse, she asks: What is the psychic price of trying to raise my kids *on the side?* What can I *gain* from walking away from job seniority and lifetime security? How can my marriage benefit from reinventing the balance of power, so that income needn't play such a large role? And what can I do, today, to change the world so my kids won't be faced by the same kind of either/or choices that have stymied and almost defeated me?

These stay-at-home moms are no fools. They know they'll re-enter the workforce at their own risk; that's the bargain they've made with life. If they do end up earning 5 to 7 per cent less than their peers twenty years hence, as Alderman promised, well — weren't those years spent with the kids worth a few percentage points? It is hard to argue with Alderman's warnings about security, and most at-home moms do struggle with this. They're not certain what's around the corner: how they'll put those kids through college, and whether they'll end up working full time at age seventy while all those long-time career women are living it up in Miami. But who can be certain what's around the corner, anyway? Careers can go off the rails, and future plans can be shredded in the blink of an eye. Ultimately, for at-home and at-work moms alike, it comes down to making the wisest choice for you and your family, for now, and doing your best at planning for an always-uncertain future.

STRATEGY #3: WORKING FLEX

A few years ago, the word "flex" was often used as a euphemism for whatever women had to do to their work schedules when their home schedules interfered. This was most likely to happen around the birth of a child, and often took the form of a phase-in period from maternity leave back to full-time work. Today, flexible work arrangements tend to be much more formalized — a corporate response to the pressure on both women and men to find time for childcare, eldercare, community work, personal development, and even secondary employment. Full-time flex options include flex day (say, a 7:00 to 3:00 shift on some or all workdays), flex week (say, four nine-hour days, or six six-hour days) and flex place (work-from-home, or telecommuting). Part-time flex options include job-sharing and a variety of shorter-day and shorter-week arrangements.

The increasing use of flex arrangements by men was documented in a study released in 1997 by Statistics Canada in its quarterly magazine, *Canadian Social Trends*. Researchers found that in many companies men have adopted flex policies with greater speed and gusto because they tend to be in the positions of power where there is greater access to change and less penalty for making it. The study noted that to make a successful transition to flex time, you've got to start with a good, full-time job. Accordingly, 40 per cent of the Canadian men surveyed reported they were using flex time, compared with 30 per cent of women; 25 per cent of men were doing shift work, compared with 19 per cent of women; and about 23 per cent of men had flex-place arrangements, compared with 21 per cent of women. Paradoxically, some of the policies implemented with women in mind (such as compressed work weeks) appear to work better for men than for women. About 21 per cent of women working a regular week told the Statistics Canada researchers that they were in a serious time crunch; that rose to 29 per cent for women working compressed weeks.

There's a disturbing circularity to the results of flex policies: Those who are in the strongest position at work are most likely to thrive under flex arrangements, but those who need them most may not get them. Human resources consultant Jane Boyd confirms this observation. The owner of Vancouver-based Work, Family & Life Consulting Services sees rapid progress in the use of flex time for both men and women in many of the large, innovative companies, and especially among employees with strong track records. At Vancouver City Savings, a client of Boyd's and one of Canada's most family-friendly firms, the five-year-old flex policies are embraced as a way to promote good work from good workers. And flex is just one page in Van City's family-friendly catalogue. Head office employees also benefit from emergency childcare back-up (for $10 a day), a private lactation room for women who want to continue breastfeeding infants in care at the attached facility, a free pager-borrowing service for employees with expectant wives or ailing relatives, and a 1,500-title family resource library.

Many professionals working in human resources are counting on corporations like Van City to lead the way to societal acceptance of flex as a workplace norm. Critics have observed, however, that while policies at these workplaces just seem to get better and better for their own workers, there is limited spillover to society. "The women I worry about are the single moms working at small companies who feel quite powerless to do anything about their work arrangements. It's a very big social problem, not just a workplace problem," says Boyd. She is an agent for Pat Katepoo's Flex Success software in Canada, and often uses it to help individual women who do not work for progressive companies.

In general, the banks are leaders in accommodating the needs of female employees — partly because they have so many women on staff, partly because they're under intense public scrutiny, but largely because they're in one of the few corporate sectors that has been making steady profits in the last five years and so it's easier for them to share the bounty. The Royal Bank of Canada, for example, has made sweeping changes to acknowledge the fact that the productivity of their workforce in previous generations has depended on workers who had someone at home to handle the family. Now, nearly three-quarters of women with children under sixteen are in the labour force — most of them part-time. The Royal Bank, like other innovative employers, therefore considers part-time options of all kinds to be a valid (if slower) lane on one's career track. More than 1,000 Royal Bank employees (of the 55,000 total) share jobs; about 1,000 more work flex time and about 600 have flex place. Norma Tombari, manager of the Royal's flexibility solutions program, says internal surveys demonstrate that such innovations significantly reduce stress among workers, leading to less absenteeism and greater productivity.

Innovation is also welcome in the booming information-technology sector. At Hewlett Packard, the majority of women on staff have opted for compressed work weeks, flex time, or part-time (with full benefits starting at twenty hours a week) — all of which reflects the impact of HP's 7,000-strong Women's Information Network. At IBM, close to 80 per cent of female employees use some kind of flex program. At Bell Canada, telecommuting is fast becoming the norm for women in middle management and sales, thousands of whom spend a good part of their week working from home. Bell is also exemplary in its extended leave options, including an educational leave program that allows employees to study for up to four years while continuing to draw 25 per cent of their salary.

This is important progress, but it is largely limited to long-term employees in the right corporations. And even in those settings, women working at levels from middle management up are loath to "jeopardize" their careers by opting for flex, according to Catalyst, the New York–based support organization for working women. In a 1993 national study of women working at the managerial and professional level of seventy companies, Catalyst found that most still perceive significant risk in opting for alternative schedules. Unless they're facing intense pressures to compromise (such as those brought on by the arrival of a baby), they aren't prepared to put their careers in jeopardy. For management and professional women, "face time" is still considered equivalent to "productive time" in most workplaces. Simply *being there* for full days and full weeks is proof that you're focused on your work. Not being there means you're not.

But the fact is, there is no such proof of productivity. Studies by Catalyst have shown repeatedly that employees who embrace flex policies are just as productive as those who don't — if not more so. For example, it is well documented that workers are most productive on Mondays because that's the first day of the week. With job-sharing, companies have effectively created two or three Mondays in each week. Shorter workdays have been proven to raise, not reduce, the daily output of employees, who are happier and more awake. Likewise, telecommuting can boost performance: A 1996 work-at-home project at Illinois Bell showed a productivity increase of 40 per cent among workers taking part.

The Catalyst researchers were therefore not surprised to find, in their 1993 study, that women who had adopted flexible arrangements were doing very well. Two-thirds of those surveyed said they would have left their companies had flex options not been available; 53 per cent had earned promotions while working flexibly. But what did surprise the researchers was the resistance they still found among the human resources professionals working at those seventy companies: One-quarter of them believed that employees who used flex policies would jeopardize their advancement opportunities.

Corporate culture obviously takes time to change, and the onus still falls largely on the shoulders of individual women who want and need that change. Which brings us to the art of negotiation. Even at companies where flex policies are formalized, employees are often obliged to earn the privilege of using them, and then are expected to show that the policies are paying off. As Catalyst's vice-president of research, Marcia Kropf, puts it, getting your company to agree to an alter-

> **It is well documented that workers are most productive on Mondays—the first day of the week. With job-sharing, companies have effectively created two or three Mondays.**

native work schedule is the easy part. Setting it up so it works well over time is the real challenge, and it demands proactive planning and positive communication among all parties. Here are four key steps to achieving a positive flex-time outcome, according to Kropf:

Show your employer how a change to flex time will improve productivity

In a written proposal to your supervisor, clearly identify your goals and make sure increased productivity is at the top. That way, your move benefits the company as much as it does you. For example, clarify which "core duties" you are better equipped to handle in this arrangement, and which can be delegated to another staffer as a "career development opportunity." By focusing on the upside of all this to your employer, you avoid the "poor-me" pitch, which is more of a plea than a negotiation and is unlikely to do much long-term good.

Take the initiative to follow up

After the new schedule is in place, meet periodically with your supervisor to assess how it's working. Be prepared to reconfigure the arrangement if necessary. "Just because your manager doesn't say anything, it doesn't mean the schedule is okay. By not discussing it, you make it an all-or-nothing proposition," says Kropf.

Take pains to communicate your new schedule with co-workers

Some co-workers may see a move to flex hours or to telecommuting as a retreat from full-time work, and may even resent you for it. Your best defence is open communication and an upbeat attitude. If you telecommute on Fridays, for example, this may strike some colleagues as a glorified long weekend. It's up to you to reinforce your full-time connection with the rest of the staff. Advises Kropf: "If they say, 'Have a nice long weekend,' you need to say, 'I'll be working at home tomorrow. Call me if you need me.'"

It's up to you to stay in the loop

You should not expect your colleagues to keep track of your schedule and plan meetings or deadlines around you. Think proactively, and plan around them. For example, if a meeting or joint project needs to be scheduled, initiate discussion well ahead of time and suggest a date for taking care of business, making it clear which days are best for you. "Let's get this started on Monday" is much more positive than "I can't do it Friday because I won't be here." Says Kropf, "People will think of you as being responsive. At the same time, you're in control because you've anticipated their needs."

Anyone approaching negotiations for flex time, or for any similar workplace arrangement, ought to approach it with equal amounts of determination and patience. These must be seen as investment strategies, to be implemented in a cautious, staged manner for maximum returns over the long run. Particularly at companies where resistance to change is high, the employee who works hard to earn the right to make incremental changes will get much further than the one who rushes in with demands or ultimatums. For example, if telecommuting is still rare at your workplace but you think you can make a good case for it, start by proposing a one-day-a-week trial, with built-in reviews at three and six months, and stick with that until you've proven how well it can work. Then move on to stages two and three — earning more flexibility and control as you go. (Catalyst offers a package of materials on work/family strategies: see Resources, page 238.)

It must be said, though, that flex time does not work well for everyone. Self-discipline is a prerequisite, particularly where telecommuting and other work-at-home options are concerned. Those who thrive in controlled environments where hours and workload are regulated often do not thrive given unstructured time and space. Not all of us are skilled at creating our own structures, or at meting out our own discipline when we fail to produce. Children add to the challenge when it comes to work-at-home options, and this is the catch-22 for parents who want flex time precisely so that they can spend more time with their families. Having your children near is one thing; having them right on top of you is quite another. Without strict limits, both your family and your job will suffer.

There are ways to make this work, as a cousin of mine knows. She works at Bell Canada, and telecommutes two days out of five in order to spend more time at home with her two young children. She has a nanny in place for the full week to keep childcare systems steady, and has been very clear with the children, from day one, that when she's working she's not on active parent duty. That doesn't mean she's out of bounds, however. (That would defeat the point of being at home.) What it means is that if her pre-school son has a minor problem or needs a hug, he has to wait for coffee break. And her six-year-old daughter knows she's welcome to bring her school work into mommy's office at 3:30 and to work quietly there, at the far end of the desk. She'll get a kiss and a wink on entering, but she knows better than to expect mommy to help her sound out a hard word. That has to wait till mom has logged off the modem and tuned back in to her kids.

If you're able to run your household like a military operation — as my cousin does and I did — flex time will probably work well for you. But if you are easily distracted, beware. Kids are an insurmountable occupational hazard for nervous moms (What's that noise? Has Karly just thrown Benji off the roof?), and even an empty house can be distracting (Should I finish these worksheets, or scrub the toilet?).

And if you've chosen flex time as an alternative to paid childcare, are you prepared for the burden of parenting in shifts? Will it bother you if your partner attends teacher interviews alone, if you handle the softball schedule, he the church fund-raisers, you the mothers' march? Will it bother your kids to find their family fractured for much of the week? What effect will this have on your marriage? Are you prepared to give up week-night dinners together? Can you break your daily routine of after-work gossip, letting off steam, or sharing news with your partner? Can you wait for midnight to touch base? Can you wait for the weekend to touch bodies? Many couples are successful at surmounting such challenges, through sheer determination and precision scheduling. But for others, the toll of constantly passing their partners like ships in the night is extremely wearing, and shift work is abandoned in favour of more traditional arrangements.

> **If you're able to run your household like a military operation, flex time will probably work well for you. But if you're easily distracted, beware.**

STRATEGY #4: SPENDING LESS

If your goal is to work less, one of the best ways to achieve it is to spend less. This is also the ticket to bigger goals, including a more equitable society and a more liveable planet. There are good reasons to spend less money, no matter how hard you work and how much you earn, because the spend-less strategy, much like the work-less strategy, makes sense on both a personal and political level. The simplicity movement invites us all to think holistically about our day-to-day consumption, and we can tear a page from their book even if we don't care to read all the way to life on $20 a day. "Can we construct an economy and culture where people are better off with less?" asks Juliet Schor. "Less work, less stress, less crime, less violence, less inequity, less shopping and less stuff. We must acknowledge this head on."

The first step to spending less is figuring out how much you're spending now, and why. This is a tough task, and many of us make ourselves very busy at work so we won't find time to tackle it. Allow me to run some numbers for you, based on an interview I did with a mid-income family that is spending every hard-earned cent they're making. I won't use my own downshifting experience for this exercise, because it was not typical. In terms of income, Shaw and I were early achievers — though I've done my best to rectify this in the last couple of years. In the early years of our marriage, we made a few smart investments, and got lucky with our timing — such as buying a house in what suddenly became a hot real estate market. As a result, we accomplished 90 per cent of our financial goals by simply moving to the suburbs. I also had the advantage of possessing a skill I'd been honing for almost two decades, and being able to market it from home. Our transition was therefore quite painless.

The young couple I interviewed are in a much tighter box. She has an entry-level management job at a public utility, working a standard forty-hour week for an annual salary of $36,000, with generous medical and dental benefits. Her husband makes $42,000 as comptroller for a small manufacturing firm, and they have two pre-school children. Both kids are in day care, which eats up $8,000. Tax gobbles up almost $20,000. Their mortgage on a three-bedroom home in a middle-class suburb costs them $13,000. Because their suburban location requires two cars to get to two workplaces, almost $5,000 goes to transportation. Other ongoing costs (utilities, insurance, basic food and clothing, medical/dental, furnishings, etc.) add up to about $18,000, barring crises such as the death of a car or fridge. Another $3,000 goes to service old debt from student loans and from an aborted business start-up. That leaves about $8,000 for entertainment, education, recreation and gifts, plus a modest family vacation in the summer, and $3,000 for a minimal contribution to college and retirement funds.

Can this family live on less? Not without making some tough adjustments. They're already living ominously close to the bone, which is exactly where many young families find themselves, and many not-so-young families. You might say they're not faring so badly, compared to those on unemployment or welfare. But it is a bind because they're exhausting themselves and can't see a way to stop doing exactly what they've been doing without throwing the delicate balance of their lives dangerously off kilter. This is the backdrop for the work-related angst we keep reading about, and the common denominator is the sense of being locked in.

So let's rework their budget. Let's say a bigger crisis strikes than the death of a fridge. The husband's company goes into receivership, and his hours are reduced to a three-day week, with a corresponding wage cut to $25,000. And let's say the young dad has a bounce-back ego and immediately sees the opportunity in this disaster. He decides to work at home two days a week, minding the kids and reinvesting some time in that old, stalled business enterprise that just might fly given some spit and polish. Finding time to think while caring for small children won't be easy, but our hero is keen to give this a try, hoping at the very least to reconnect with his kids, and at best to find a long-needed escape hatch from a job whose appeal is diminishing daily. But how to make ends meet? Going back to the bank is not an option. They simply have to cut $17,000 from their household budget.

It takes our young couple one very long evening with a calculator, tax tables, and lots of coffee to rework their finances. What they find is that day care can be cut by $3,000, with dad at home part-time plus some support from a neighbourhood child-minding cooperative. Taxes will drop by almost $4,000, but $2,000 will have to be ploughed back into start-up on the new company. In year two, they'll see some benefit from the tax deduction of start-up losses, but let's stick with year one here. The house can be remortgaged, for an annual savings of $3,000. Gas savings and maintenance on one car will net them close to $1,000. On faith, the college fund can be put on hold ($1,000), the clothes budget frozen, Starbucks banned, and restaurant lunches replaced by brown-bag specials ($2,000 total). With a bit of weekend handiwork, the rec room can be transformed into living space for a foreign student ($5,000). And there you have it: $17,000 to the good, and a future that no longer looks quite so bad.

There are countless ways to reach a similar end, depending upon your resources, ingenuity, and level of comfort with risk. If you have no rec room to rent out, or no house of your own to remortgage, you might need to consider cashing in a chunk of your precious retirement savings plan to get you through a tough couple of years. Some accountants will say this is very bad advice, but only you (and your own accountant) can properly make that call once you've measured the gains against the tax penalties. Your best move depends on your current financial position, your future career prospects, and the state of the economy. If your retirement funds are netting low annual returns, for example, they might indeed be better spent rebuilding your career instead of waiting for you to retire from it.

But those are extreme measures, and most of us can find significant savings simply by trimming fat. The sad fact is, a lot of fat is often attached to a household's second income — which is a real slap in the face for those of us who feel forced to keep bringing in those dollars. In their book *Staying Home*, Darcie Sanders and Martha M. Bullen point out the steep cost of having two parents in full-time jobs. Restaurant lunches, take-out dinners, dry-cleaning, house cleaning, yard work and keep-busy activities for children can easily eat up a third of the second income, say Sanders and Bullen. Take tax out, and how much are we actually adding to the pot at the end of a workday?

Maybe you're not as locked in as you thought. This is not wishful thinking — it's *detail* thinking. And as my good friend the accountant constantly tells me, your financial future is all in the details. Just as work expands to fit the time allotted to it, expenses have a tendency to grow right to the end of your bank manager's wits. The first step in saving money is taking ownership of your spending, away from your bank manager, the advertisers on TV, and the Joneses next door. Drawing up a detailed budget will put you way ahead of all those hardworking people who say they don't have the time to sit down with a calculator. And your first reward in spending less is the knowledge that you are resilient, that you can weather retrenchment and reinvestment, and that you're capable of setting your own priorities. (For more help, see the downshifting worksheets at the end of this chapter.)

STRATEGY #5: SEQUENCING

Who among us knows exactly what lies around the next bend? Change is the only constant in life, and this truth underlies a way of living that we can either choose or have thrust upon us. Choosing to live this way gives us a leg up because we are then navigating those shifting seas rather than simply bouncing from one wave to the next, ever fearful of an approaching tsunami. Such a choice allows us, in effect, to plan for constant change — which may sound like a contradiction in terms, but isn't. This is not the kind of planning that attempts to pin everything down and label it, like so many dead butterflies. This is a more open-ended form of planning that gives breathing space to fate — or fortune, or misfortune, or sheer possibility, whatever fits your notion of the future. There's a dash of chaos at the centre of such planning, which is what gives it its vital flexibility. Many people plan this way by nature. They are the optimists: They're able to bounce back from catastrophe and roll with success. If you've taken the test at the end of Chapter Two (Check Your Career Transition), you'll know where you stand and how hard you'll have to work on this.

Sequencing is the latest buzzword for this open-ended approach to life and work, but you can call it what you want: serial retirement, mid-course correction, living your life in "chapters." A good friend of mine, Robin Pascoe, calls it "yo-yo work-ing," and she's a consummate practitioner. A journalism grad with experience in broadcast and print, Robin has rein-vented herself a dozen times in as many years, thanks partly to having married a foreign service officer. With two young children in tow, she has followed her hus-band Rodney from Ottawa to Bangkok,

> **When it comes to respond-ing to change, women have an edge. We bend over backwards to accom-modate the diverse demands of our busy lives.**

Taipei, Beijing, and Seoul, then back to North America, where she has lived on two coasts and worked on three (a news assignment from a Winnipeg TV station found her trekking the Arctic tundra at Hudson Bay). Her most challenging career moves were made while abroad, where governmental conflict-of-interest rules prevented her from working in the media. She turned to teaching, ran support work-shops for women, and wrote two well-received books — humorous survival guides for ex-patriate wives and families.

"It's true that my choice of marriage partner impacted profoundly on my career choices," she told me,

> but I have always managed to turn what others might see as a negative into a positive. It is because I have been forced to reinvent myself every few years that I have a résumé others envy. Of course it helps that I am a high-energy person. I thrive on having a lot of balls in the air at once, and moving around from country to country has just made all those balls more interesting. In all, I don't think that I could have asked for a better career path. It's certainly been a lot more inter-esting and challenging than if I had stayed in one place. If I was still doing television news today, fifteen years later, I think *that* might be depressing. It would mean I wouldn't have grown professionally at all.

When it comes to responding to change, women have an edge. This is probably due to a variety of factors: our bodies are constantly surprising us with change; children have a way of arriving at the oddest times; our husbands, parents, and friends all stake their various claims on our time — and we cope with it. We bend over backwards to accommodate the diverse demands of our busy lives; we juggle, and keep moving forward. We understand that life is both long and short: long enough to allow us to bounce back from virtually anything; too short to be spent doing only one thing. And so we embrace change as the means of having it all — if not all at the same time.

Men, it seems, have more choices but tend to use fewer of them. Very often, they make one career choice early on, and get stuck there until someone or something takes it away. Though this is a simplistic analysis, there's enough truth in it to explain the trouble so many men have had in these last years of corporate downsizing. According to career counsellors, women have weathered the storm of workplace change significantly better than men, achieving a higher rate of success in relocation.

To be fair, it's not that men are averse to change. It's more a case of social expectation. "It's because of all the stuff they carry with them," says Rita Morin, a senior career consultant with KPMG in Vancouver.

> Men are more often the breadwinners, and that makes it harder for them to see change as an opportunity. They're more likely to see it as a catastrophe — where is the next pay cheque going to come from? They want to turn around and send out three hundred résumés and get another job right away — which of course doesn't work any more. Today, it's all about networking, retraining, getting yourself positioned for the right job.
>
> Women seem to be more open to alternatives. And that's not just because someone else is there to support them. We see this even when the woman is the breadwinner. There's more openness to trying something different, maybe starting

up her own business, or going back to school. Women are also much more likely to take advantage of the services we offer to get themselves recharged. There's a healthy willingness to ask for help.

Sequencing is not a euphemism for delayed gratification, though it is sometimes used that way by working mothers who take "time out" to raise a family. In fact, the time-out notion defeats the spirit of sequencing, which is about finding joy and meaning in all the different kinds of work that we do over the course of our lives. Amanda Siegel, a thirty-four-year-old Indianapolis mother of two who left her law practice just after the birth of her first baby, bristles at the idea that taking time away from her career is any kind of sacrifice. "I am not *out of work*," she's quick to point out. "Frankly, I think this job is much more important (and more difficult) than working as a lawyer or a judge. There is nothing more important to the human species than raising our young to be the kind of people we want them to be."

On the afternoon I spoke with her, Amanda had just finished a craft project with her son, Jonah. "The things he thinks of," she marvelled. "He picked up an egg carton and ripped off a piece and said, 'this is an airplane, I fly my airplane.' Well, actually, a foam egg carton can make a pretty decent airplane. I wouldn't have thought of doing it, but he did. So I obliged, and created a fuselage, and wings, and weighted the thing, and we had a blast!" Amanda is entirely fulfilled by making planes with Jonah, nursing her infant, volunteering at her synagogue, and reading everything she can get her hands on. "Life is really pretty happy," she says.

> When I was a lawyer, I found intellectual fulfilment through other avenues — mostly reading cases, meeting with and learning about clients and trying to solve their problems, thinking about the law, reading legal magazines to integrate them into my understanding of the law. I still read the

Supreme Court digests as they come out — you can join a mailing list for that, and I do enjoy keeping up to date. This will help when I start working towards my judgeship.

Amanda expects that her husband, Miles, a research chemist for Eli Lilly & Co., will be pleased to see her return to the workforce. "He married a woman he thought was a career lawyer. It's not so much the financial concern, as the sense that our marriage is a bit off balance, that we're not sharing the parenting and the breadwinning evenly. But we'll get back to that, in time." Amanda's self-confidence goes a long way to explain her indomitable happiness. Her sequencing game plan involves a long stay at home, at least till her children are in high school, followed by a return to law, probably as public defender or prosecutor — a common route to a bench appointment. It doesn't bother her that she might be sixty-five before she gets that judgeship. Age doesn't faze her, which is another essential asset for sequencing. In this, she's inspired by her mother, who, at seventy, sold one of two businesses she owned and operated, and plans to keep the other one going until she's eighty. "Then she's going to go live in one of those retirement communities that look like such fun."

EX-FILE | *The Tent Dweller*

NAME: Wanda Barrett, 47

EX: Computer analyst

CURRENT: Artist, teacher, workshop facilitator

RÉSUMÉ HIGHLIGHTS: Arts degree; early work as computer programmer and systems analyst; later as elementary school teacher, special education consultant and art therapist

PERSONAL: Divorced; two children

BACKGROUND: I made my decision when I was eighteen. I could have had a career in San Francisco, as a computer programmer with Pacific Gas and Electric Company. I was working there and putting myself through college. But I felt I had to make a choice — between a very interesting, creative life of soul or a life of business. Back then, I saw these as separate (I don't see it that way now, but when you're young it's very black and white). I chose the inner riches over the outer riches, and this choice has informed my whole adult life.

I have been willing to live more rustically than most people are willing to live, but what I get is freedom, and to me it's worth it. I have always had a garden and grow a lot of my food. I tend to have very low housing expenses one way or another — I've been pretty creative that way. I always have wood heat in my home, and I like to get my own wood and split it, and I do a lot of my own building and maintenance work. If there are things that I need that I can't afford, I barter. I try to avoid the need for very much cash in my life. I know where to harvest fruit. I make my jams and preserves from wild berries. I seek out people in my community I can work with and trade with. All this allows me to work at part-time jobs, and have time for my family and my creative work, and to have good variety in what I do every day — lots of physical, outdoor work as well as working with people and sitting down at a computer. To me, that makes a rich life.

CRISIS AND SOLUTION: Last Christmas my fiancé died unexpectedly. I faced the prospect of going back to work full-time, because I had been depending in part on his income. I was paying rent for a house [on Bowen Island, near Vancouver], and my daughter was going to a private school — I could not continue paying the bills. What I decided to do was basically what I've done many times over the last thirty years. I reduced my biggest expense, which was housing. When I lived in California, I spent years almost rent-free, caretaking people's places where there were animals at risk or where the land could get trashed for lack of anyone being there. I would do work on the property, keeping it up, building bridges over creeks, tending trees, and making gardens.

But I've always wanted to build a house of my own. Not a big house, and definitely not one that would burden me with a mortgage. When I saw what an Oregon company was doing with prefab yurts, it struck me as ideal. Yurts are a form of temporary shelter that the Bedouins use, traditionally; they're made of canvas on a wooden or earth foundation. The ones that Pacific Yurts manufactures are beautiful round structures, insulated with a high-tech material developed by NASA. I approached friends on Bowen and they agreed to let me live rent-free on their property and build the yurt for them. They would use it seasonally as an art studio. It's basically a living/eating area, plumbed in the kitchen, and we've built adjacent sleeping cabins which use wood heat, as the yurt does. We use the bathrooms in the main house. I bought the yurt for about US $10,000 US, and my friends are gradually buying it back from me, which means they're paying me to live here, on their property. It's a wonderful arrangement for all of us, and I'll end up saving probably $9,000 a year, after tax.

TAKE-OUT WISDOM: I've learned a lot by looking at tribal cultures. When you see the faces of people living in Third World countries, you may see poverty but you often see happiness too. When I look at the faces of people in our civilized Western world, where we work so hard and put so much emphasis on work, our faces show a real struggle. We're not happy, most of us. I feel we can live better than this. We can do both: We can be in the Western world, using technology to minimize the amount of time and work necessary to our survival and maximize our time for creativity and joy.

The kind of simplicity I believe in is connected with beauty and integrity. Many times, people equate simplicity with poverty and even squalor. I believe there is another paradigm: that you can live very simply but everything you have is beautiful and high quality. We live in a very comfortable, pleasing way. It's not a punishing kind of life at all. I mean, most people aim to live this kind of life when they retire, when they look for the best possible way to use their limited resources well: to make them last, and do what they want with their hard-earned money. They wait all their working lives till they can enjoy themselves like that. It seems a shame to have to delay what a lot of us can have much sooner.

EX-FILE | *The Self-Marketer*

NAME: Susan Freedman, 54
EX: Communications manager
CURRENT: Marketing consultant
RÉSUMÉ HIGHLIGHTS: Advertising copywriter and editor, The Bay, 1964–75; producer, director, communications manager at CBC Alberta, 1975–91; marketing director of The Fringe theatre festival, Vancouver, 1995–present.
PERSONAL: Married; four children, three grandchildren.

BACKGROUND: I took Arts at the universities of British Columbia and Manitoba but spent most of my time involved in drama and musical theatre and never graduated. It has taken me years to rediscover my passion for live production. In the interim, I fell into advertising, moved on to research at the CBC and then up to various production and management positions. By

1984, having moved to Edmonton for a promotion, I was the only female director of radio in the corporation. I moved up to communications manager just in time for the first round of major job cuts at the CBC. Mine was one of 1,200 to be eliminated.

It was a real heartbreak. I loved working for the CBC, even if my later years in management were far too focused on how to make the unending budget cuts. After my job ended there in 1991, I just couldn't see myself turning around and getting back into the corporate world. We had moved to Edmonton from Calgary for that job, and were considering moving back when I heard about someone else whose job had been cut and who was sailing, long term, in the Caribbean. I had dreamed for years of taking a leave to go and live in London, so why not now? After amazingly little discussion, Bill and I decided to go for a year. Our kids were in university or working, and our parents were in decent health. We sold our house, had a giant garage sale, and put a ton of stuff in storage. In July 1991 we took two huge suitcases each and flew to London.

THE HIATUS: London was fabulous. We rented a furnished flat on the fifth floor (88 steps!) of a Georgian building on Harley Street. We walked everywhere. We saw as much theatre as we could, plus galleries and music. I took classes at the Central School of Speech and Drama where I had dreamed of going when I was eighteen. I knew that I would go back to Canada before long, that I would need to work and that I wanted to be able to do so more independently than I had before. If I was going to freelance I knew I would need to feel confident that my skills were broad and current. I enrolled in a program given by the Communications, Advertising and Marketing Education Foundation — the professional body that sets standards for communications curricula and examinations in the UK. It took two years to get my certificate, after which our one-year trip had turned into an almost three-year sojourn.

We agreed it was time to go back to Canada, but where

in Canada? We had no house and no jobs. Three out of four of our children (plus a beautiful new granddaughter) lived in or around Vancouver and like many Albertans, we had spent all our family vacations in BC. In May of 1994 we moved into a rented apartment in Vancouver.

THE MAKE-OVER: Having no business contacts in Vancouver apart from CBC, which was still under siege, I knew I would have to start from scratch. But I did have several hours remaining of the outplacement counselling that was part of my CBC package — I'd only used a few hours before leaving for England. I had mailed the company (Drake Beam Morin) the odd card while I was away so they wouldn't forget me — I knew I'd need them when I got back. This was one of the most valuable experiences I've had. They put me through lots of tests and exercises all focusing on my values, my interests, my successes. There was much emphasis on what I liked and didn't like in all my past jobs, and what an ideal job would be for me. My counsellor helped me home in on a job, and plan my presentation. I had never worked freelance, and hadn't looked for a job for almost twenty years.

At CBC in Edmonton I had been very involved in setting up our sponsorships of arts organizations in the community. My favourite was The Fringe theatre festival — Edmonton's Fringe was the first, and is still the biggest, in Canada. After attending some plays at The Fringe in Vancouver I called Joanna Maratta, the festival producer and founder (I got her name out of the program) and told her I didn't think they were getting nearly the support from the community and the media they deserved, and I said I could help make that happen. We met, I made a formal proposal and ultimately convinced them to hire me as marketing director.

I'm now heading towards my fourth year with the Fringe and I love it. I spend about seven months of the year working on the festival, but it's part-time, which leaves opportunities for other marketing contracts — including with CBC. I will never make the kind of money I made when I was on staff, but we have no debt and we simply don't spend money like we did when we were both working full-time. [Husband Bill Galloway, a lawyer, has recently returned to university to take a Masters in Liberal Studies.]

I work at home, which is complicated, but for me there are more pluses than minuses. There's always a load of wash to put in, a meal or a personal phone call to make — the distractions are always there. But I find an hour worked at home is a more productive hour than at the office. There is no catching up with everyone after the weekend, no wading around forever in office politics. There's also no colleague at the next desk to bounce ideas off, so it can be a bit isolated, but I love setting my own work patterns and seem to thrive on the independence. I get little work done in the mornings and quite a lot done in the evenings. And I will probably never buy another suit.

When I first arrived in Vancouver I had "head shots" done because I was thinking seriously about getting back to acting. Somehow I got into marketing again instead, but acting is still on my mind. Perhaps the next chapter....

TAKE-OUT WISDOM: There really was a silver lining for me in the black cloud of CBC cuts. It made me feel less reverent towards my jobs in general and less uptight about big changes. In my next life, though, I would try to remember that the place you work is not your mother. I'd always keep a bag packed.

 **CHECK |**
Your Financial Sense

1. **MAKE A PIE CHART**
   a) The first step in making a budget is to look at the way you're spending your money now. Get out a pencil and some paper,

and start by adding up what comes in and what goes out monthly, estimating where needed:

Family income, after personal taxes _____

Shelter (principal and secondary homes) _____

Food (groceries and restaurant meals) _____

Childcare _____

Transportation (cars, repairs, insurance, commuting expenses…) _____

Clothing, dry-cleaning _____

Health and personal care (medications, therapies, grooming, dental…) _____

Insurance (health, household, life, disability…) _____

Recreation (trips, equipment, lessons, hobbies, books, music, pets) _____

Education (tuition, courses, supplies) _____

Household maintenance, furnishings _____

Savings and retirement (including in-trust for children)

b) Compute the percentage of each expense category as a portion of after-tax income, then draft a pie chart to give yourself a rough picture of your household budget. If you have basic accounting software, your computer will do this for you. If not, use quick-and-dirty freehand. To give you some perspective, here is what a Canadian financial planner considers to be a typical

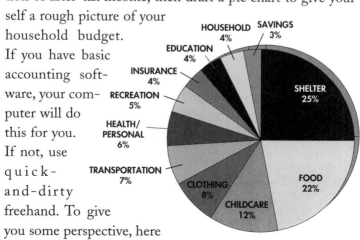

middle-class family's budget (two parents, two children, one-and-a-half incomes, suburban location).

2. REDUCE YOUR BUDGET

Once you know what you are spending, you're in position to find savings. In their book *Your Money or Your Life*, Joe Dominguez and Vicki Robin suggest the surest route to savings is figuring out how long it takes you to earn each dollar that you spend. This is a real eye-opener, especially for women who are bringing in that "extra" income in relatively low-paying jobs. Say, after taxes, you net $500 a week for which you work 40 hours. That's $12.50 an hour. Or so it seems. But look at your pie chart and estimate how much you are actually spending in order to earn that wage — in terms of transportation, childcare, restaurant meals, clothing, and work-related entertainment. If day-care is involved, this can easily add up to $250, so you're really netting $250 a week, or $6.25 an hour. Now consider that you have to spend time to prepare yourself for work, to get there and back, to catch up on weekends, etc. You may in fact be working 50 hours to earn that 40-hour-a-week wage, which brings your net earnings down to $5 an hour.

It takes you a full hour of work, in other words, to buy a take-out lunch. Worth it? That depends how much value work holds for you at this time in your life. If your goal at work is to invest in your long-term career, to keep up your skills and contacts and level of challenge, it probably is worth it. But if you're only working for the money, this little exercise will help you put the right value on your time and effort. Is there a way to add value to your time and effort? Would cost-cutting give you the flexibility to work less without much financial penalty? Once you know what your work is costing you versus what it's netting you, it's much easier to answer these questions.

One way to add value to your work time is to do more than one job — at the same time. This is the key to success in the new work world, say many career counsellors. Instead of looking at our work lives sequentially (we do this job for three years then move to the next one, or we do this job in the day and another one at night), it's much more productive to juggle a variety of work responsibilities at once. Because women are so good at juggling, we're well suited to the new work paradigm. While we are at the office, our creativity can be working for us at home — or in another office. Consider some options:

■ Does your regular work afford the opportunity of a spin-off business or service that can be done with your employer's blessing, utilizing office time and resources? A few years ago, this sort of arrangement was considered a conflict of interest. These days, it's considered creative. If there's something in it for both of you, why not negotiate?

■ Do you have interests or skills that you're not utilizing at work? Consider setting yourself up in a home-based business, even if you're nervous about cash flow. These days, the set-up is as inexpensive as you are resourceful: Shop at office liquidation centres; beg or borrow equipment from friends; use curtains or portable dividers to create space; join a child-minding co-op to create time. (There are several good self-help books on this subject.)

■ Do you have an extra room in your house that can be rented to a student? Or consider renovating — even a tiny, self-sufficient suite will bring in double the rent of a room.

■ Can you increase your earning power by bartering for basic goods and services for which you are now paying? Many communities have bartering exchanges such as LETS (Local Employment and Trading System) which mix and match trading partners. Look for contacts in community newspapers, co-op stores, libraries, and community centres.

Resources for Change

My own approach to making a major change is to stall for as long as possible. I read everything I can and talk to everyone I know, then winnow it down to what I consider real wisdom. In my books, there's no better way to spend time. To change directions we have to shift gears: it's neither smart nor safe to negotiate those hairpin curves at full speed. When we take the necessary time, we can better enjoy the fallow stage of life. This is our soul's respite.

Such opportunities to *pause* don't come very often in a lifetime, and in the scheme of things they hardly last more than a moment. Make it last. Don't treat it as work. Research ought to be undertaken not as an assignment, but as an escape — into the world of possibilities. Be willing to entertain ideas that seem far-fetched at first. Consider, for example, ideas about work that bear little or no resemblance to your notion of productivity; ideas about success that don't require a "goal." Sounds weird to you? Open your eyes and your mind, suspend judgement and before long a clear picture of your own best options will likely emerge.

"Next" is not simply your next job, though that will probably be a part of it. This book's view of next is more holistic — a better way of living that incorporates a better way of working. For that reason, these resources combine broad approaches to life change along with more focused discussions of work. Increasingly, these days, vocational counsellors are taking this kind of approach with their clients — urging an exploration of personal values and passions as part of the vocational search. This is how one arrives not only at a job, but at meaningful, sustainable work. It may be necessary to continue doing "just a job" while we search for our life's work. What's critical is that one knows the difference, and keeps searching.

This is not to say you shouldn't rest until you've found paying work that will save the planet and redeem humanity. Indeed, when we speak of "meaningful work" we should be clear that meaning often lies more in the way you work than in the job you do. Jacob Needleman, the American philosopher and author whose book *Money and the Meaning of Life* is included on my list, argues for a return to the old values — the ones that rewarded a person's ability to "make his own way" and to "stand on his own feet."

"But now," writes Needleman, "more and more people yearn for work that is in itself 'meaningful.' They feel unable to bear the psychological stress (the 'hell') of a job — especially in an office — when the reward is 'only' money. People want to serve some greater good, some immediate human need — *and* get paid for it." Where money used to be seen as a means to support ourselves in life, we now see it as an end — and a nasty one at that. We earn it, and feel soiled by it — unless we're reducing the hole in the ozone while we're at it.

So demonized has money become that, like Faust, we think we're selling our souls to the devil when we enter the market place. Says Needleman: "Isn't it obvious that it is nobler to assist the poor, to teach children, to help save the environment, than it is to write advertising copy, say, for a high-tech electronics firm, or to plot marketing strategies for a new line of soft drinks, or to manage investment portfolios for the rich?" Yes, it's obvious. But it's not true, he says, because we've got "noble" all wrong. *Inner* freedom is what we ought to be striving for: freedom from ego-driven power plays that can cause much harm in the name of *doing good*. "Who does more good — a man or woman with inner freedom selling a pair of shoes, or a madly self-righteous prophet blind to all the humanly destructive effects of his *good deeds*?"

Ultimately, what is meaningful for me is rarely meaningful for you, because it comes from deep inside. If this book, and the resources list below, help you on your way to self-discovery, then I have accomplished my goal — which was never to change the world, after all. I just wanted to write this book, and hoped a few readers would get something out of it.

BEST IN BOOKS

On Inspiration, Motivation, and Soul Food

Ageless Body, Timeless Mind, by Deepak Chopra, Harmony, 1993

The best-selling author of *Quantum Healing* and *Perfect Health* combines ancient mind/body wisdom with current anti-aging research to show that there is nothing inevitable about aging — that through our innate healing powers we can retain physical vitality, creativity, memory, and self-esteem.

Care of the Soul: A Guide for Cultivating Depth and Sacredness in Everyday Life, by Thomas Moore, HarperCollins, 1992

Drawing insight from classical mythology, philosophy, and his own work as a therapist, Moore urges self-acceptance more than self-improvement, and does so eloquently. This book is a spiritual salve for those stressed by the non-stop demands and hectic pace of working life.

Do What You Love, the Money Will Follow, by Marsha Sinetar, Dell, 1987

By evaluating and identifiying sources of self-esteem, and banishing negative "shoulds" as identified in this book, readers can work on getting over their resistance to change and move on to success on their own terms. Don't be scared off by the platitudes — there's some valuable advice here.

Emotional Intelligence, by Daniel Goleman, Bantam, 1995

Goleman, a psychologist and science writer for *The New York Times*, combines anecdotal and scientific research to show how our rational and emotional faculties work together to shape intelligence. He cuts the old IQ theories down to size, offering a much wiser view of what it takes to achieve success and happiness.

The Heart Aroused: Poetry and the Preservation of the Soul in Corporate America, by David Whyte, Currency-Doubleday, 1996

Whyte is a poet turned consultant who helps corporate clients bring creativity back into the boardroom. It works on a personal level as well. Employing elegant language and resonant images, this is a seductive little book that makes some sharp points.

I Could Do Anything If I Only Knew What It Was, by Barbara Sher, Dell, 1994

No one sugar coats motivation better than Sher, or writes with more warmth and personality about the basics of self-discovery. What do you really want, and how are you going to get it? This is a follow-up to her hugely successful *Wishcraft*, and it's even more spunky.

Live the Life You Love, by Barbara Sher, Dell, 1996

If you liked *I Could Do Anything*, pick up this step-by-step guidebook and put Sher's method to a road test. Can she turn you from a dreamer into a doer in ten easy steps, as promised?

Living Without a Goal: Finding the Freedom to Live a Creative and Innovative Life, by James Ogilvy, Currency-Doubleday, 1995

A philosopher and business consultant, Ogilvy teaches us how to "make it up as we go along" — letting go of the tyranny of our goal-driven lives in order to pursue personal creativity and freedom.

Meditations for People Who (May) Worry Too Much, by Anne Wilson Schaef, Ballantine, 1996

This is a graceful sequel to Schaef's *Meditations for Women Who Do Too Much* — also a collection of daily thoughts and anecdotes. Schaef helps us to smile at our worries, to re-examine our discontent and to get over our desperate need to control our lives.

Money and the Meaning of Life, by Jacob Needleman, Doubleday, 1991

By addressing money as a key to the question of who we are, and drawing on personal experiences and mythical figures, the author explores our fears and fantasies about money, the cost of our needs, and the price of being time-poor.

New Passages: Mapping Your Life Across Time, by Gail Sheehy, Random House, 1995

In this sequel to her blockbuster *Passages*, Sheehy extends her inspirational message about finding strength and meaning in life's journey through the years: from the "flourishing forties" through the "flaming fifties," menopause, serenity, and wisdom.

The Princessa: Machiavelli for Women, by Harriet Rubin, Doubleday, 1997

Patriarchy is dying — and not a moment too soon, says Currency-Doubleday president Harriet Rubin, New-Age diva of business publishing. Her intriguing new book inspires and empowers women to take full advantage of today's shift in the balance of business power.

The Soul's Code: In Search of Character and Calling, by James Hillman, Random House, 1996

"We need a fresh way of looking at the importance of our lives," writes psychotherapist Hillman, and in his new book he delivers just that. His "acorn theory" proposes that each life is guided by a spirit/destiny, and by finding and following it we can find answers to this fundamental question: "What is it, in my heart, that I must do, be, and have? And why?"

Time Shifting: Creating More Time to Enjoy Your Life,
by Stephan Rechtschaffen, Doubleday, 1996
The author believes that time is subjective, not objective, and people can take back control of their lives by changing the way they think about time. Both inspiring and useful, this book helps readers imagine how they can live fuller lives.

Your Money or Your Life: Transforming Your Relationship with Money and Achieving Financial Independence,
by Joe Dominguez and Vicki Robin, Penguin, 1993
Dominguez and Robin helped launch the simple-living movement with this little book, and still use it to help many people figure out the difference between making a living and making a life. There's advice on getting out of debt, taking stock of values and priorities, tuning in to social and environmental activism, and more.

On Feminism and Family

Children First: What Our Society Must Do — and Is Not Doing — for Children Today, by Penelope Leach, Alfred A. Knopf, 1994
The childcare guru turns her rhetorical skill to politics, making a powerful and extremely well-researched argument for fundamental changes in how society values and cares for children.

The Feminine Economy and Economic Man: Reviving the Role of Family in the Post-industrial Age, by Shirley Burggraf, Addison-Wesley, 1997
An economist, a feminist, and a parent, Burggraf examines the opportunity costs of raising children, and in so doing uncovers the deep damage wreaked by an economy that devalues traditional women's work.

The Feminine Mystique, by Betty Friedan, Dell, 1984
First published in 1963, this is the book that ignited the sexual revolution. Read it for social history, but also for the message

that remains relevant — a call to arms against ongoing marginalization of women by economic and political power structures. (For more reading on the evolution of the women's movement and the ongoing struggle to find fulfilment at work and at home, read Friedan's *The Second Stage* and her most recent book, *The Fountain of Age*.)

Feminism Is Not the Story of My Life, by Elizabeth Fox-Genovese, Doubleday, 1996

The central dilemma in feminism is examined: the conflict between a woman's prerogative to live independently and her biological/emotional role as mother. Fox-Genovese offers her prescription for a renewed "family feminism" that would replace divisive politics with inclusive pragmatism.

Homebase: A Forum for Women at Home, a quarterly publication of The Nonprofit Association Mothers Are Women (MAW). This home-grown Canadian journal is a networking and support vehicle for at-home moms, and the voice of a nascent movement to bring value to the unpaid work moms do at home. Edited in Ottawa, it is more of an open forum than a magazine, giving voice to opinions and concerns of women who work at home. Contact MAW at (613) 722-7851.

Talking from 9 to 5: Women and Men in the Workplace: Language, Sex and Power, by Deborah Tannen, Avon (paperback), 1994

The author of the popular *You Just Don't Understand* offers fascinating study of how men and women talk at work, and how it affects their ability to thrive there. It all starts at the watercooler, but goes much deeper.

The Time Bind: When Work Becomes Home and Home Becomes Work, by Arlie Russell Hochschild, Henry Holt & Co., 1997

Thoroughly researched, eloquently written, this is a welcome addition to Hochschild's growing canon of social criticism (previous best-seller: *The Second Shift*). She employs anecdotal journalism to analyse the new work order and describe its frightening toll on families.

Working Fathers: New Strategies for Balancing Work and Family, by James Levine and Todd L. Pittinsky, Addison-Wesley, 1997

Directors of the Fatherhood Project at New York's Families and Work Institute, Levine and Pittinsky have written an informative and highly practical guide for fathers who are struggling to fill both breadwinning and parenting roles. More like this, please!

On Vocational Change

Boom, Bust & Echo: How to Profit from the Coming Demographic Shift, by David Foot and Daniel Stoffman, Macfarlane Walter & Ross, 1996

This is one of the best sources of trend-smart ideas for anyone interested in doing business in Canada today. Unlike some of his American counterparts, Foot favours fact over jargon in his presentation of demography as a powerful tool to help us turn market forces to advantage.

Breaking Out of 9 to 5: How to Redesign Your Job to Fit You, by Maria Laqueur and Donna Dickinson, Peterson's Guides, 1994

Practical guidance on redesigning your work schedules. Laqueur and Dickinson offer helpful descriptions of the new workplace options (permanent part-time, job-sharing, compressed weeks, flex time, telecommuting) followed by clear advice on how to negotiate such alternatives and to maintain your career focus.

Business Capital for Women, by Emily Card and Adam Miller, Macmillan, 1996

Though very American in scope, this book contains numerous

helpful strategies that Canadian women can use in tapping financial sources to start and develop a company. It includes an excellent reference section on women's business associations and non-profit support groups, as well as statistical information on women in the workforce.

Canada's Best Employers for Women: A Guide for Job Hunters, Employees and Employers, by Tema Frank, Frank Communications, 1994

Self-published by an enterprising Toronto business consultant, this little handbook is based on a massive research project the results of which will be of interest to every job-hunting Canadian woman. If your bookstore doesn't stock it, ask them to order it from Frank. In the United States, each October *Working Mother* magazine publishes its "100 Best Companies for Working Mothers" (also available on Women's Web; see next section).

Career Intelligence: Mastering the New Work and Personal Realities, by Dr. Barbara Moses, Stoddart Publishing, 1997

Author of the widely used *Career Planning Workbook*, human resources consultant Moses has written a new book to help people take charge of their lives and position themselves to thrive in the new workplace. It includes valuable self-marketing tools and advice on preparing for areas of competence rather than for jobs, and is also useful for parents interested in "career-proofing" their kids for the next century. At bookstores or by phone: 1-800-668-9372.

Clicking: 16 Trends to Future Fit Your Life, Your Work, and Your Business, by Faith Popcorn and Lys Marigold, HarperCollins, 1996

If you don't mind seeing the word "clicking" in every other sentence, you'll find real value here. The indefatigable Popcorn surveys the market place and comes up with myriad suggestions for entrepreneurial pursuit.

The Complete Canadian Small Business Guide, by Douglas
and Diana Gray, McGraw-Hill Ryerson, 1995
Here is a well-crafted book filled with practical, step-by-step
advice on starting and managing a small business in Canada. It
includes street-smart tips, sample forms and checklists, plus information on how the new entrepreneur can obtain government aid
and other start-up resources.

**The Consultant's Calling: Bringing Who You Are to What
You Do,** by Geoffrey Bellman, Jossey-Bass, 1990
Just what is a consultant, anyway? Bellman offers answers, show-
ing how to turn your personal strengths into marketable skills. Also
provides useful tips on handling conflicts and dilemmas common
to consulting businesses, including professionalism and ethics.

Excelerate: Growing in the New Economy, by Nuala Beck,
HarperCollins, 1995
A best-seller in Canada, this is a well-organized guide to finding prosperity in today's market place. Beck, a prominent
Toronto business consultant, uses a star rating system to track the
strength of virtually every sector of the economy, from waste
management to candy manufacturing. Watch for a new US edition.

The Female Advantage: Women's Ways of Leadership,
by Sally Helgesen, Currency-Doubleday, 1990
Helgesen describes the outstanding careers of four American
women to give inspirational heft to her thesis that women make
great leaders in today's business world. Though the focus is on
superachievers, there are lessons for all of us — including men.

**The Feminine Quest for Success: How to Prosper in
Business and Be True to Yourself,** by Nancy Bancroft,
Bennett-Koehler, 1995
This book approaches Helgesen's theme but from a broader per-
spective, analysing the differences between men and women in

their approaches to success and fulfilment. Bancroft defines the five basic business styles of women —Trooper, Emulator, Balancer, Seeker, and Integrator — and invites readers to find their match.

How to Find the Job You Really Want, by Janice Weinberg, Henry Holt and Co., 1994

This is a highly practical guide offering direction to career seekers in the changing economy. It includes advice on getting to the interview and how to handle it, as well as a very thorough list of American contacts and sources.

The Job/Family Challenge: A 9 to 5 Guide, by Ellen Bravo, John Wiley & Sons, 1995

Ellen Bravo is Executive Director of 9 to 5, the National Association of Working Women. Based on workshops with employers and employees across the US, including thousands of people who call 9 to 5's Job Problem Hotline, Bravo offers excellent advice on handling maternity or family leave, dealing with childcare and sharing of household duties, and negotiating for family-friendly work alternatives. Very useful to Canadian readers, despite some references to American law and policy.

JobShift: How to Prosper in a Workplace without Jobs, by William Bridges, Addison-Wesley, 1994

This is among the most radical of career guides, thanks to Bridges' no-nonsense approach to personal change. The business consultant and best-selling author provides strategies for "getting over" the old job-for-life thinking and moving on to prosperity in contingent, temporary, and self-employed pursuits.

Making a Living While Making a Difference: A Guide to Creating Careers with a Conscience, by Melissa Everett, Bantam, 1995

Not the most practical of guides for job seekers, this is nevertheless a must-read for Canadians who want to get off the traditional career track to take up work they can feel passionate and proud about. Includes lots of real-life offerings from people who work with conviction.

100 Best Careers for the 21st Century, by Shelley Field, MacMillan General, 1996

A comprehensive listing of the jobs of the future, including salaries, educational requirements, and a summary of duties and skills. One of the best features is the extensive inventory of associations and contacts for information on the career fields discussed in the book.

101 Best Businesses to Start, by Sharan Klahn and the Philip Lief Group, Doubleday, 1992

Virtually everything you need to know about starting up your own business, from estimating costs to assessing risks, plus real-life success stories. This revised edition includes a section on environmental businesses.

The Overworked American: The Unexpected Decline of Leisure, by Juliet B. Schor, Basic Books, 1991

This oft-quoted text by radical economist Juliet Schor inspired and continues to inspire many activists in the Shorter Work Time movement. Schor makes her case against modern American-style capitalism with hard research and compelling rhetoric.

Put Work in its Place: The Complete Guide to the Flexible Work Schedule, by Bruce O'Hara, New Star Books, 1994

O'Hara, who is Canada's leading Shorter Work Time advocate and who works a thirty-hour week as a vocational counsellor, offers this how-to sequel to his first book on the same subject, *Working Harder Isn't Working: How We Can Save the Environment, the Economy and Our Sanity by Working Less and Enjoying Life More*, also from New Star Books.

Resumes for Women, by Eva Shaw, Arco Publishing, 1995

A tidy little book that answers more questions than most of us would think to ask about writing a résumé. Using seventy-five sample résumés from successful women in every field, Shaw deals with questions of childcare, maternity, and eldercare leave, dealing with a spouse's relocation, etc.

Teaming Up: The Small Business Guide to Collaborating With Others to Boost Your Earnings and Expand Your Horizons, by Paul Edwards, Sarah Edwards, and Rick Benzel, J. P. Tarcher, 1997

The latest from Tarcher's popular "Working From Home" series, this one helps home-based entrepreneurs reach their goals by teaching them how to effectively reach out. Extensive research from interviews and focus groups is quoted, and strategies are laid out for combating isolation and boosting business.

What Color Is Your Parachute? by Richard Nelson Bolles, Ten Speed Press, revised annually

There's good reason why this is the top-selling job-hunting book in the world. Nelson Bolles makes career planning a science, and self-assessment fun! (Well, almost.) In addition to his very readable text, there are illustrations, charts, an appendix, and a contact list to help you network your way to job satisfaction.

Work and Family: The Crucial Balance, Ontario Women's Directorate, Ministry of Community and Social Services

A tidy resource guide for employers looking for proven strategies that promote work-family balance. It is also a useful lobbying tool for employees making a case to employers based on the documented benefits achieved by companies such as the Toronto Blue Jays, Xerox Canada Ltd., and Levi Strauss. Free in Canada, by phoning (416) 597-4570.

Women Breaking Through: Overcoming the Final 10 Obstacles at Work, by Deborah J. Swiss, Peterson's Guides, 1996

The awkward title belies the real practicality of this book, which surveys 325 mid- and senior-management women in a wide variety of fields to uncover the strategies they've used to overcome obstacles. Through personal accounts, we learn how these women restructured male/female business relationships, created informal communication channels, took risks, battled sexual harassment, and triumphed in the end.

Working From Home: Everything You Need to Know About Living and Working Under the Same Roof, by
Paul and Sarah Edwards, G.P. Putnam's Sons, 1994
Practical advice on everything from physically setting up the office to staying focused, managing your time, dealing with friends, and juggling family responsibilities. Value added: a survey of home-business opportunities, with the pros and cons of each.

Working Woman; Working Mother; and Ms., Lang
Communications, New York
This fine trio of news-stand magazines covers nearly every social, political, financial, and even recreational concern of working women, though kids do get the short end of the stick. If you're wired to the Internet, check out Lang's excellent site, Women's Web (see below).

BEST ON THE WEB
It's easy to get lost for hours searching for job information, resources, and contacts on the Internet — but that's no reason to stay away. It's simply reason to be smart about your search, to know what you're looking for and how to get there quickly. The smart place to start is one of the women's Web sites, such as Women's Web or Women's Wire. They all have some form of work department, from which you can glean expert advice, survey personal/political/social perspectives on workplace issues, get connected to live forums and chatlines, peruse job postings, and get linked to other Web sites offering similar services. Yes, this can take days if not weeks to navigate, but it's time well

spent. While you're not likely to find a job (unless you're in a high-tech field and can travel), you almost certainly will make contact with other women who are in your position.

Cyberspace, once the domain of young male nerds and porn junkies, has become an enormously exciting place for women to hang out, make friends, and do business. Which is not to say that money necessarily changes hands. It's more a case of opening doors and minds to a world (both virtual and real) of opportunity. Surveys show that women overwhelmingly use the Net for research relating to jobs, pastimes, and courses of study, while men tend to use it for entertainment and news. And while many women start out browsing the Net, most end up spending the larger part of their time on e-mail correspondence, either one on one or as part of an e-mail list. I'm typical in this regard. I found my feminist moms' e-mail group through the Feminist Mothers at Home Web site (see following under "Cosmic Woman Pages"), and now I tend to do most of my Internet business and socializing through e-mail channels. It's more personal, more private, and easier to keep track of e-mail files. Because the women on my list are savvy browsers, I tend to bounce back into the Web on the recommendation of my list sisters — going straight to the best sites.

I've tended to avoid books on using the Internet, because I end up bogged down in the books and losing valuable learning time on the Net. If you prefer learning from books, however, there are a number of good guides for beginners, including *The Internet for Dummies, The Official Netscape Beginners Guide to the Internet,* and *Canadian Internet: New Users' Handbook* (Prentice Hall, 1996), all of which cover the basics of browsing, e-mail lists, newsgroups, and general troubleshooting. There are also books dealing specifically with electronic job searches. Among the best I've seen is *Be Your Own Headhunter Online,* by Pam Dixon and Sylvia Tiersten (Random House, 1995). It covers all the nuts and bolts, from posting your résumé to creating your own home page, surfing the Net, and the art of online networking. For Canadian entrepreneurs interested in enhancing small and home-based businesses through electronic networking, Jim Carroll and Rick

Broadhead's *Canadian Internet Advantage* (Prentice Hall, 1997) is an extremely well-packaged guidebook.

But there is no instruction half as good as simply getting out there, pointing and clicking and stumbling your way across the wires. Listed below are my favourite "links" to women's Web sites, some of which are little more than a glorified path to other links. Though Web sites have a tendency to come and go, my selection favours those with a solid track record and a steady volume of visitors.

The Web for Women

About Work, part of the American *ivillage* group,
http://www.aboutwork.com
A sleek, chat-oriented site, with departments covering first jobs, career planning, and working from home, plus a cathartic "Bitch & Moan" forum ("Coworkers from hell," "Revenge Fantasies," and the like). The day I dropped by, a colourful line-up of hourly chats were scheduled, including how to raise start-up money, pros and cons of retraining, and online job searches. Coaches and facilitators are on hand to keep things rolling.

Canadian Women's Internet Association,
http://www.women.ca
A national non-profit association whose goal is to "take back the net" by providing a safe, welcoming community for Canadian women. Excellent links to government resources, vocational experts (get to Nuala Beck's home page from here), job sites (*The Globe and Mail's* Career Connect; Canada Employment Weekly, etc.), plus e-mail lists for Internet novices, women in business, and at-home moms seeking connections.

Cosmic Woman Pages,
http://www.millcomm.com/~pvallen/cosmicwoman
Cosmic Woman is Ann Allen, an American net whiz and stay-at-home feminist mom whose home page is a handy link to some

of my favourite sites for women and parents. Allen is a charter member of Wise Women of the Web, another rich networking site offering support, inspiration, and creative outlets for stay-at-home and work-at-home moms. She is also owner of the Feminist Mothers at Home e-mail list, which is cyberhome to 135 wired women from around the world.

Full-Time Dads, http://www.parentsplace.com/readroom/fulltdad
This New Jersey–based support group for at-home fathers publishes a free newsletter to help members stay current on parenting issues. It also offers a well-used forum for discussion and artistic expression. Book reviews, poetry, social advocacy, and hot links for dads.

Home-Based Working Moms, http://www.hbwm.com
A membership fee of US $34 buys you a subscription to this Austin, Texas–based association's monthly newsletter, *Our Place*, which is a useful on-paper guide and networking tool for mothers (and fathers) who are working at home or would like to be. The Web site also offers advice on setting up and marketing your home-based business, avoiding pitfalls, dealing with tax and accounting issues, juggling household responsibilities, etc.

National Organization for Women (NOW),
http://www.now.org
An excellent, frequently updated site for American feminism, with news, analysis, a bookshop, and links to a broad range of feminist resources on the Net.

Parentsoup, http://www.parentsoup.com
Another fun site from ivillage, the American company behind *About Work*. This one is just as sleek and chat-filled. You can join the discussion any time of night or day, on topics of broad interest to moms and dads. When I dropped in, chat topics included home-schooling, first-time grandparenting, alternative medicine, frugal living, and singles support.

Pleiades Networks, http://www.pleiades-net.com

California-based site offering a solid Internet introduction for novices as well as a popular discussion forum with topics on career, parenting, finances, relationships, health, etc. Click on the Women's Directory for links to hundreds of Web sites for women. Click on "work" for US funding sources, career networks, and business/ professional support organizations. An internal search engine helps you navigate the links.

Today's Parent, http://www.todaysparent.com

Online version of Canada's best-known parenting magazine offers timely chat topics, a pen-pal exchange, a message board, and frequently asked questions on parenting, plus hot links to other Canadian and US parenting sites.

Women's Connection Online, http://www.womenconnect.com

Less a home page than a well-organized bank of databases, including magazine articles, bulletin boards, and directories (many of them hot-linked to this site) geared to women in business, especially those in entrepreneurial fields.

Women's Resource Directory (WoRD),
http://www.ghgcorp.com/wordweb

Online version of the Houston-based non-profit organization that publishes an annual professional directory of American women in business. Expert opinions and links are provided to meet members' needs for start-up marketing, mentoring, legal, and insurance services. A series of Referral Exchange Roundtables promotes the women-helping-women mandate.

Women's Web, http://www.womweb.com

The joint site of three women's magazines published by Lang Communications of New York: *Working Woman*, *Working Mother*, and *Ms.* Editorial content, like the magazines, is very high quality, but there's much more here than reprinted stories. Check out the women's events calendar, the "Job Alert!" and *Working Woman*'s interactive databases: The Top Women-Owned Companies and The Hottest Careers for Women.

Women's Wire, http://www.women.com

Graphically gorgeous and commercially laden (to the point that it downloads at glacial speed), it's nevertheless worth a visit to see state-of-the-art Web site design. Not nearly as much to read as to see, but Biz Shrink is fun and useful (she's a job counsellor who hangs out under the "Work" banner) and the chatlines are a riot (under "Buzz"). Oddly enough, *Working Mother* magazine's annual listing of "The 100 Best Companies for Working Mothers" is included on this Web site, not on *WM*'s own. Go figure, but do go there!

WWWomen WebRing, http://www.webring.org

Not so much a site as a linking service, offering an online tour of hundreds of women's Web sites. The folks who operate this ring are on the ball, keeping commercial intrusions and pointless diversions to a minimum, with the result that this ring is a browser's paradise, providing you have a little time on your hands.

ASSOCIATIONS FOR SUPPORT & INFORMATION

- Alberta Women's Enterprise Initiative Association, Edmonton, AB, tel: (403) 422-7784 or 1-800-713-3558, e-mail: aweia@compusmart.ab.ca
- American Association of Black Women Entrepreneurs, PO Box 13933, Silver Spring, MD 20911-3933, tel: (301) 565-0527
- American Association of Home Based Business, PO Box 10023, Rockville, MD 20849, tel: 1-800-447-9710, fax: (202) 310-3130
- Business Women's Network, a division of the Public Affairs Group, Washington, DC, tel: (202) 463-3773, e-mail: ernetti@tpag.com
- Canadian Federation of Independent Business, 3555 Don Mills Road, Unit 6-105, Willowdale, ON, M2H 3N3, tel: (416) 534-7324,

fax: (416) 537-2545; bid request line for federal contracts: 1-800-361-4637, or (613) 737-3374 within Ottawa

- Canadian Women's Foundation; Women and Economic Development Consortium, #504-133 Richmond St. W., Toronto, ON, M5H 2L3, tel: (416) 365-1444, fax: (416) 365-1745
- Catalyst, 250 Park Avenue South, New York, NY 10003, tel: (212) 777-8900
- Clearing House on Women's Issues, PO Box 70603, Friendship Heights, MD 20813, tel: (202) 362-3789 or (301) 871-6101
- Entrepreneurial Mothers Association, 375 E. Elliot, Suite 2, Chandle, AZ 85225, tel: (602) 892-1464
- Environmental Career Opportunities, PO Box 15629, Chevy Chase, MD 20825, tel: (301) 986-5545
- Formerly Employed Mothers at the Leading Edge (FEMALE), Elmhurst, IL, tel: (708) 941-3553
- Indigenous Women's Network, c/o Winona LaDuke, White Earth Land Recovery Project, PO Box 327, White Earth, MN 56591
- Institute for Women's Policy Research (IWPR), 1400-20th St. NW, Suite 104, Washington, DC 20036, tel: (202) 785-5100
- National Association for the Cottage Industry, PO Box 14850, Chicago, IL 60614, tel: (312) 472-8116
- National Association for Female Executives (NAFE), publishers of *Executive Female* magazine, 127 West 24th Street, New York, NY 1001, tel: (212) 645-0770
- National Association of Mothers' Centers (chapters in most US states and some in Europe), tel: 1-800-645-3828 or (516) 520-2929
- National Association for the Self-Employed, 2121 Precinct Line Road, Hurst, TX 76054, tel: 1-800-232-NASE
- National Association of Women Business Owners, 1100 Wayne Avenue, Suite 830, Silver Spring, MD 20910, tel: (301) 608-2590, fax: (301) 608-2596
- 9-to-5 National Association of Working Women, 614 Superior

Ave. N.W., Cleveland, OH 44113-1387, tel: (216) 566-9308, toll-free job survival hotline: 1-800-522-0925 or (216) 566-9308 within Cleveland

- National Chamber of Commerce for Women, 10 Waterside Plaza, Suite 6H, New York, NY 10010, tel: (212) 685-3454
- Non-traditional Employment for Women, 102 East 22nd Street, Room 710, New York, NY 10010, tel: (212) 420-0660
- Shorter Work-Time Group, US, c/o Barbara Brandt, #1-69 Dover St., Somerville, MA 02144, tel: (617) 628-5558, URL: http://www.swt.org
- Shorter Work-Time Network, Canada, c/o Bruce O'Hara, Box 3483, Courtenay, BC, V9N 6Z8, tel: (250) 334-0998, e-mail: boh@mars.ark.com
- Women and Economic Development Consortium, c/o Canadian Women's Foundation, 133 Richmond St. West, Ste. 504, Toronto, ON, M5H 2L3, tel: (416) 365-1444, fax: (416) 365-1745
- Women's Resource Directory (WoRD), P.O. Box 66796, Houston, TX 77266, tel: (713) 242-0908, fax: (713) 242-9578, e-mail: wordweb@ghgcorp.com, URL: http://www.ghgcorp.com/wordweb
- Women to Women Communications (publisher of international listing of women's magazines), PO Box 161775, Cupertino, CA 95016
- YWCA, check your closest location

Paula Brook has worked in the magazine industry for eighteen years, most recently as editor-in-chief at *Western Living*. She has earned awards for both her own articles and for her magazines. Paula Brook lives in Vancouver with her husband and two daughters.